101 AMAZING THINGS YOU CAN DO WITH DOWSING

MAGGIE PERCY

NIGEL PERCY

CONTENTS

ALSO BY MAGGIE & NIGEL PERCY

Dowsing Ethics: Replacing Intentions With Integrity

The Practical Pendulum Series, Volumes 1-4

Pendulum Proficiency: You Can Learn To Dowse

How To Dowse Accurately & With Confidence

Dowsing Pitfalls & Protection

Dowse Your Way To Health: An Introduction To Health Dowsing

Dowsing: Practical Enlightenment

The Dowsing State

Ask The Right Question: The Essential Sourcebook Of Good Dowsing Questions

The Dowsing Encyclopedia

The Essence Of Dowsing by Nigel Percy

The Credibility Of Dowsing, edited by Nigel Percy

Healing Made Simple: Change Your Mind & Improve Your Health

Dowsing Box Set

Dowsing Reference Library

Space Clearing: Beyond Feng Shui

Caring For Your Animal Companion: The Intuitive, Natural Way To A Happy, Healthy Pet

Busy Person's Guides

The Busy Person's Guide To Energy Clearing

The Busy Person's Guide To Space Clearing

The Busy Person's Guide To Ghosts, Curses & Aliens

ISBN: 978-0-9978816-6-0 (Ebook version)

ISBN: 978-0-692-38164-9 (Paperback version)

Sixth Sense Books

PO Box 617

Chino Valley, AZ 86323

www.sixthsensebooks.com

To Michele Fitzgerald, a dear friend and respected colleague who is an expert dowser and intuitive.
Thanks for the idea for this book!

We suggest you visit Michele's website at http://sedonaportal.com.

PREFACE

Dowsing is a valuable natural skill that can extend your intelligence immensely by giving you answers to questions you cannot answer using your rational mind. No doubt the ability to focus intuition and get accurate, fast answers without having to think long, logically and linearly saved many of our ancestors from danger in Nature, but as society became more 'civilized', it came to value science and those things it could see, explain and measure, rather than intuition and the way it leaps to answers.

There will always be people like us who use dowsing simply because even though we cannot scientifically explain exactly HOW it works, we have seen it work so many times that we need no additional proof. What matters most to us is that dowsing extends our ability to create positive outcomes in our lives. And we want to share dowsing with anyone who is interested in changing their lives for the better.

This book is organized to take you from simple to more challenging dowsing topics. It will give you a lot of ideas for using dowsing in very practical ways. You can skip around, but if you are not a confident, practiced dowser, you will have better results starting at the beginning and working through in the order presented. Detachment and practice are required for success in more challenging topics like health. And we put unverifiable topics at the end, because if you can't check your answers, it isn't a learning experience. We also put concepts like energies and the future at the end, because they are more challenging subjects to get your head around.

This book is NOT a dowsing course. We have included some dowsing basics in this book, but it is not intended as a teaching guide, so we recommend that you visit our website and check out our Discovering Dowsing course (http://discoveringdowsing.com/dowsing-course). Dowsing is a natural skill anyone can learn, but like the skills of playing a piano or riding a horse, it's far easier to learn from a human instructor than from a book. Our course is loaded with videos that will teach you proper techniques and useful applications. Visit http://discoveringdowsing.com/dowsing-course and use the coupon code 'save15' (without quotes) to save 15% on the Discovering Dowsing course—available on discs or thumb drive.

Maggie Percy

January 6, 2015

What Is Dowsing?

Your Untapped Intuitive Potential

You have physical senses. You can see, hear, smell, touch and taste. Your senses give you information about your environment. They help you make safe and productive choices.

You also have intuitive senses. These are not spoken of in Western culture, but they are addressed in aboriginal cultures, which have a closer relationship to the natural world. Native American tribes believed you had intuitive senses that were analogous to your physical senses, but had different functions. Your intuitive senses help extend your information-gathering ability to make your life safer, more productive and more successful. So it pays to use them.

Dowsing is a skill for tapping into your intuitive abilities. Dowsers ask questions, usually in yes/no format, to get information they cannot get rationally. Looking for the best spot to drill for water using dowsing is a good example of an application of dowsing and how it extends your ability beyond the rational.

Dowsing isn't like some psychic power that you have full access to at birth. Sometimes you stumble on it rather late in life, as we did. Either way, it doesn't matter. You can learn this powerful skill and transform your life with it. Just about anyone can learn dowsing, though some people pick it up more quickly and easily than others. It requires training to become good at it, just as you'd need training in any other skill.

Dowsing is unique, in that it is a Whole Brain activity. You have two sides to your brain. The left brain functions more in the rational realm of logic and linear thinking. The right brain excels at creative and intuitive leaps. Both sides are valuable. If you use all your cerebral abilities, your life can be far more successful.

Unfortunately, in our society, the left brain is valued far above the right brain. But you don't want to live with one arm tied behind your back, do you? Why not use ALL your brain power? Learning to dowse is an activity that brings your right brain online and helps you tap into your intuitive potential.

There are many ways to engage your right brain and intuition. Channeling, tarot card reading, palmistry, meditation, visualization and other methods are very helpful in building intuitive 'muscle'. But dowsing is the only method we know of that uses BOTH left and right brains to tap into your intuitive potential. As such, it is attractive to a wider variety of people, seems less like a flaky, freakish psychic activity and has more credibility in terms of daily use.

You have untapped intuitive potential. Dowsing is the best way to unleash that power and see positive change in your life.

How To Dowse

Let Maggie & Nigel Teach You Dowsing

Our DVD course will help you master the skill of dowsing, no matter what your level of experience. For details, visit http://discoveringdowsing.com/dowsing-course.

Special Resources

You'll get more out of this book if you take advantage of the free resources at our website, Discovering Dowsing, at http://discoveringdowsing.com. We have loads of multi-media resources we couldn't include in this book. You will see videos on how to use each type of tool, how to dowse without a tool and articles on various dowsing applications, plus videos of presentations at national meetings.

This book is just an introduction to some of the many ways dowsing can be fun and improve your life. At Discovering Dowsing, you will be able to dive deeper into this fascinating subject. When you finish the book, be sure to check out the Resources section near the end for still more help.

Learning To Dowse

I remember one time going to work in a carpool with a very impatient driver who constantly tailgated people. On two occasions, he had rear-ended people because of that. Yet one dark morning driving to work, he exited the parkway behind a service truck and suddenly allowed his speed to go way down, so that he fell back some distance from the truck, exactly the opposite of what he usually did. Suddenly, a ladder that had been lashed to the side of the truck fell off onto the road and landed exactly where we would have been if he had not slowed down so uncharacteristically. When asked why he had done that, he said, "You aren't the only person who gets intuitive hits."

Almost everyone has had the occasional experience of just 'knowing' something and not being able to say why. You may have been certain someone was lying to you, or you felt sure that a situation was dangerous and you should not do something. Later, your insights were proven to be correct. But you brushed it off, because you couldn't explain it. That's your intuition, and it usually operates randomly, giving you 'hits' and 'gut feelings'. Dowsing is different, because you focus on a particular subject you want an answer about, and you get it. There's nothing random about it. It's focused intuition.

Dowsing is a natural skill, and as such, you need training and practice to become good at it. Just as anyone can learn to make music or play a sport, anyone can learn to dowse. And just as there are some people who learn a skill faster than others or excel at it for no obvious reason, a small percentage of people excel at dowsing.

Dowsing is not magic in any form. It is not a psychic or freakish ability. There are some basic things you need to learn in order to dowse. And then it's a matter of practicing to get better at it.

Dowsing does NOT require a tool of any kind. You may associate a tool with dowsing, because you've seen pictures of a water-witcher with a forked branch or Y-rod. Or else you've seen a friend with a pendulum. Those tools are merely used as indicators to help make it easier to see the answer to your question. But they are not required, nor do they give the answers.

No one can say for sure where the answers come from. But dowsing is not channeling answers from advanced beings. Your answers are not coming from someone else. Some people like to picture it that way, but although we cannot prove it wrong, we do not feel it is correct. It would not go along with the concept of dowsing being a natural skill if that was how it worked. The answers to your questions exist, even if you aren't aware of what they are. Dowsing puts you in touch with them. It's natural to think that because you weren't aware of the answer, that someone else must have given it to you. But that is not necessarily a logical conclusion to make. Instead, we see dowsing as using faculties different from logic to reach out and get the answer.

Whatever you picture as the mechanism of how dowsing works, the important thing is to use it to make your life better. Don't just play around with it like it's some parlor game. Don't use it to show off. Use it to create greater harmony, health and happiness in your life.

This book is not a book on teaching you to dowse. Please see the Resources section for books and websites that will help with that. But we will cover some of the basics in this book, so you can understand enough about dowsing to get started right away if you wish.

The Dowsing State

In order to access the answers to your question through your intuitive senses, you get into an altered type of state called the dowsing state. It is unique. You can picture it as a sort of combination of meditation, which clears the mind of emotion and stills it, so that you can hear the answer, and a laser focus on the question and nothing else, which connects with the answer. Simply being in a meditative state isn't dowsing and won't work. Focusing on a question while your mind is busy is likewise not dowsing. But if you can still and empty your mind while focusing on nothing except your question, that is the key to the dowsing state.

It is necessary to be in what is called a 'dowsing state' if you want to get answers to your dowsing questions. Sadly, too many courses are focused on tool use, giving the students the impression that the answers come from the tools, and all they need to know is what is 'yes' and what is 'no'. And the dowsing state never gets mentioned. People who swing a pendulum without being in a dowsing state will not get consistently accurate answers, and they are not dowsing. A large percentage of people are disillusioned with dowsing, because they are not able to be accurate. If you don't get proper training in this skill, you won't be any good at it.

It is very hard to describe the dowsing state or teach people how to achieve it, yet it is perhaps the single most important part of learning to dowse. It takes practice, so start by dowsing only in quiet places by yourself where there is no skepticism or distraction. Then, as you become able to attain a dowsing state, you can begin to dowse in public or around people. As with any skill, practice makes perfect. It may look like a Master Dowser has an easy time surrounded by many distractions, but that focus comes from many years of practice. Don't compare yourself to someone who has more experience than you. Be patient and persistent, and you will master dowsing.

How can you tell if you are in a dowsing state? It's probably easier to say when you are not. If you are feeling strong emotions or want a certain answer to your question, you are not in a dowsing state. If you are thinking about anything except your dowsing question, you are probably not in a dowsing state.

The dowsing state must be approached with a curious attitude. You are curious to find the answer to your question. But that is all. You are not emotionally attached to a certain answer. You are not concerned about being 'right' or 'wrong'. If you cannot be merely curious, you won't achieve a dowsing state.

Learning to meditate and becoming detached about life in an appropriate way will make it easier for you to get into a dowsing state. To get into a dowsing state, you have to relinquish control. If you are left-brain dominant, you may be a bit of a control freak. You may be very uncomfortable at the concept of letting go of control during dowsing and allowing the actual answer, whatever it is, to come through. You may be concerned that you will have to act on the answer, and you don't want to promise to do that unless you can be assured of what it will be. But dowsing won't work that way. Dowsing teaches you to let go of control, to become detached and to empty your mind during dowsing.

Getting into a dowsing state may require you to change a lot of things, and if it does, it will be all to the good.

Asking A Good Question

New dowsers often like to check foods or supplements to see if they are beneficial. Their first question is often quite short and simple: "Is this supplement good for me?" They are thrilled, because as dowsers, they have the possibility of getting an answer that is meaningful. A good answer will save money and give the results they want. How cool is that?

It's so tempting to grab a pendulum and start asking questions so you can get answers. Don't. Even if you have practiced the dowsing state and feel pretty confident about it, wait just a little longer. Because your dowsing answers are no better than the questions you ask. And the above question is a bad dowsing question. Sadly, most people never learn how to ask proper dowsing questions.

You see, we don't like to admit it, but humans are pretty sloppy thinkers. Some of us have particular challenges that way. We may have been taught to be specific with our words. We may understand the theory of good communication. But when it comes down to it, we prefer to use as few words as possible. We know what we want. We get impatient having to explain things in gory detail. We talk almost in shorthand and don't realize how often we are misunderstood. As a rule, we get away with doing that most of the time.

But that won't work in dowsing. To get accurate answers, you must formulate a good dowsing question. That takes time and thought. That means looking at what your goals are and defining terms very carefully and clearly.

A good dowsing question includes who, what, where, when, how and why, as appropriate. As such, a good dowsing question is usually long. You will carefully define your terms instead of assuming what they mean.

A better dowsing question would be created after considering your reasons for taking the supplement. Something like: "If I take that brand of that supplement as directed for 90 days, will it cure the headaches I have been having on the right side of my head, so that I no longer get them, if I don't change any other factors?" Notice how long that question is. Think about how removing any of the phrases could cause your answer to vary. Can you see what has been added to make sure the answer is to the REAL question you have in your mind?

But what if the REAL question in your mind wasn't about a particular symptom you want to cure? What if you just wondered if that supplement would be beneficial in some general fashion? The problem with vague questions like this is that you know supplements are good for you. You know you need them. By definition, they supply things your body cannot manufacture. And so in most cases, you'll get a 'yes' for Vitamin C (or most any supplement) being beneficial for you. But what if the 'yes' is a 2 on a scale of 10? Do you really want to spend money on something that will give you only a slight advantage? Do you have that much money to throw away?

You need to think about what results you want. Even if it isn't the eradication of a symptom or imbalance, you need to be clear as to what level of significance will compel action on your part, or be worthy of it.

One of the big changes you will see if you become a serious dowser is that you will become more conscious in how you live. You will naturally think more about what your goals are in any given situation. You will be better able to express yourself verbally. That's because in order to dowse well, you need to be able to create a good question, and knowing what you intend helps you to become better at manifesting positive outcomes.

In this book, we will give you ready-made questions that will improve your chances at getting accurate answers. But we want to make it very clear that you need to take time to ask really detailed and specific questions when dowsing. See the Resources section for books and materials on learning to dowse if you want to become a better dowser.

Tools Or Not?

Dowsing With Tools

The most commonly used dowsing tools are the pendulum, the Y-rod, L-rods and the bobber. Each has its particular strengths or weaknesses in terms of using it for dowsing applications.

We've mentioned that tools are not required for dowsing. Therefore, it follows that it isn't the tool that is doing the dowsing or giving you the answer. A tool is just a tool. There is no magic about a tool, and it is not necessary to have any ritual surrounding your dowsing tools.

So what are the strengths of each tool? A pendulum works well for dowsing over charts, map dowsing and a lot of health dowsing. Y-rods are used when dowsing for water and minerals and underground pipes. L-rods are used outdoors also, as they are more stable in wind and while you are walking than a pendulum is, and they are easier to handle for most people than a Y-rod. A bobber may be used much as a pendulum is, but also has the stability outdoors of an L-rod. It's all a matter of choice.

Pendulums are the most common dowsing tool, followed by L-rods. It's easy to make your own pendulum with a 3/4 inch metal nut and a bit of dental floss. You can bend metal coat hangers to make L-rods. If you want sleeves on the L-rods, the body of a Bic-type pen work well. You don't need to spend a lot of money or invest in fancy tools. Use tools that feel comfortable and work well for you. Remember, a tool is just a tool.

Any lesson will show you the yes/no response for the particular tool you are using. Our Discovering Dowsing site, at http://discoveringdowsing.com, has videos that are quite useful in this regard.

But there's also something called….Deviceless Dowsing

For this, you don't really need any tools at all. A dowsing tool is a device. So, no tools equals deviceless dowsing. There are many types of deviceless dowsing. Kinesiology, which is used by many chiropractors, is a type of deviceless dowsing. Our Discovering Dowsing website has a variety of articles and videos on several types of deviceless techniques. We particularly like blink dowsing, which uses the movement of your eyelids for the yes/no responses. Sounds strange, but it works!

Deviceless dowsing is terrific, because it helps you to realize dowsing is natural, that the tool has no magic, and it gives you the privacy to dowse anywhere, even in public, without anyone knowing. Check out our website for some techniques at http://discoveringdowsing.com.

The Body Sway

We strongly recommend you learn at least one deviceless technique well, so that you can dowse anytime, anywhere. Here's a brief description of the Body Sway, which most people are able to master.

Stand with your feet shoulder width apart. Relax. Empty your mind. Adopt a curious attitude. You are curious about getting answers. You don't care what they are. You make no judgments. You aren't trying to guess what they will be, nor do you feel tested. You only ask about things you cannot know rationally. This is the way to get answers.

But to test the body's polarity and your dowsing response, you can start with a question you know the answer to. Focus on the question, "Was I born in _____(your correct birthplace) in this life?"

See what your body does. It may react slowly at first. Most people find they are pulled forward. That is the usual way you get a 'yes' answer to a question.

Now ask, "Was I born in _____(name a city or country you were NOT born in) in this lifetime?" See what your body does. Most people find it eventually moves backward, which is the most common 'no' response.

Find out your 'yes' and 'no' response by asking these questions. Then, you can start each dowsing session by dowsing these questions and making sure your 'yes' and 'no' responses are not reversed. If they are reversed, that has to do with your body's polarity being reversed, and it needs to be corrected. Visit our website and enter 'polarity' into the Search box for more information on this subject.

When you are new, it may take time to get the answer, and the answer may be faint. That is because you are not focused clearly or maybe are having difficulty being in a dowsing state and quieting your mind. With practice, it gets much easier.

Now that you know your yes/no responses, you can use this dowsing technique anywhere. If you are new to dowsing, practice in a quiet, safe place a lot before trying to dowse in public around distractions. Your response will become stronger and faster over time.

Visit http://discoveringdowsing.com for faster and less obvious types of dowsing without tools!

Scales & Charts

Yes and no are valuable answers when you couldn't imagine getting them rationally, but after you've been dowsing for a while, you begin to feel a bit restricted at always having to ask simple yes/no questions. Sometimes you want more detailed answers than just yes or no. For any big or costly decision, like buying a new car or moving to a new location, you want to be sure that your choice is clear. If you use scales, you see the big difference between a 'yes' that is a 2 out of 10 and a 'yes' that is a 9 out of 10. Suddenly you've expanded the power of your dowsing.

Similarly, for charts, you can expand the range of possible choices you have. When it isn't just either/or, but instead you have a choice of 12 options, suddenly dowsing becomes more powerful.

Charts

Chart dowsing is quite popular, because it allows you to get answers when you may not have a clue what the options are. You buy a book of charts that have been created by an expert, and then all you have to do is dowse over the chart to get a very good answer. Another benefit of using a chart is that it expands the number of possible answers you can get, way beyond what you might be able to come up with yourself on short notice.

You can even make your own charts up, if you like. (Charts should always include 'other' as an option, because no one can list all the possible answers to any question. If you get 'other' as the answer, that will require more thought and dowsing in order to get to a concrete answer.) Overall, charts are very useful and can help you gain confidence in your dowsing faster.

Scales

Scales help you get shades of answers that differentiate between a strong and weak yes or no. Using a scale of 0-10, for example, you can see just how intense the pain your dog is feeling is, with 0 being no pain and 10 being the most she could feel. A scale of +10 to -10 is useful when dowsing about something that can be either deficient or in excess, like a vitamin or mineral. A mild deficiency of -1 doesn't require attention, but a -9 deficiency probably is causing health issues. You can also use the +10 to -10 scale for determining the effects of the environmental energies in your home on you or a pet. Negative numbers would obviously mean detrimental effects, while 0 would be neutral and any positive number, beneficial.

You can see that scales extend the usefulness of dowsing tremendously. But you might wonder how to dowse with scales, since dowsing is to answer yes/no questions. In a sense, dowsing can point you to the right answer about any question beyond yes and no as long as there are a list or group of possible answers.

Suppose you are using a pendulum to dowse a chart or a list of supplements for your health. The pendulum can give the answer by pointing at the right item on the chart or list. (The next section will discuss list dowsing, which is a lot like chart dowsing, but just using lists of possible answers.)

Asking a question that requests the level in effects of some energy or something can yield an answer along any scale, as the pendulum can point to the correct number. (The term 'level in effects' simply refers to how a given option will affect you on the scale you are using.) You can use a picture of a scale so your pendulum can point out the answer after being started in a neutral swing. (A neutral swing is motion that is neither 'yes' nor 'no'. It gives your pendulum momentum, making it easier for it to indicate the answer.) Or you can do it without visual scales by asking yes/no questions like, "Is the answer 8 or higher on a scale of 0 to 10? Is it 9?" You just keep asking until you get a 'yes' for a particular number.

While dowsing using scales might appear not to be a yes/no type of question, it really is. You will find short cuts to make it faster, but at first, you may want to ask the same question for each number in the scale. For example, if the question is:

On a scale of 0 to 10, with 0 being useless and 10 being the most help, how useful would a personal trainer at this time be for accomplishing all the health goals I have listed? 10? 9? 8? Just keep repeating each number slowly until you get 'yes'. That's your number.

You can also alter the question to ask if something is over an 8 on a 0 to

10 scale, because 8 is the number we suggest for taking any kind of action. So if something is 8, 9 or 10, you will act. If not, you won't. So you could ask the same question like this:

On a scale of 0 to 10, with 0 being useless and 10 being the most help, would hiring a personal trainer at this time be 8 or greater overall for my fitness goals?

There are many ways you can use scales to give you shades of yes and no and increase the value of your dowsing.

When using deviceless dowsing, as we do most often, your body's yes response will tell you when you are saying or pointing at the item on your list or chart that is the answer to your question.

As you become a better dowser, it becomes faster to use scales and charts, and it is most satisfying to get the detailed information they offer. Please visit the Discovering Dowsing website listed in the Resources section for further details on scale and chart dowsing, including videos on methods.

List Dowsing

Often you will find yourself faced with many choices when you need to make a decision. A list of items on a menu; bottles of wine lined up on a shelf; supplements listed in a catalog are a few examples. When there are too many choices to easily dowse by asking the same question over and over, list dowsing is the way to go.

This book is not a training manual for dowsing technique, and we recommend that you use the Resources at the end of this book to delve deeper into this subject. But we need to refer to list dowsing periodically in this book, and so we include a brief discussion of the topic.

You can do list dowsing in many ways. Deviceless techniques are usually easiest, because when dowsing lists, you may be in public or have the desire to have at least one hand free. You can point your finger at the page where the list is, or at the row where the bottles are lined up, and slowly moving your finger down the page or along the row, think or say your question out loud, asking to get a 'yes' response when you are pointing at the best answer.

If you have more than one page to survey or more than one row of bottles to test, first ask which row or page the best item is on that meets your criteria. We suggest that before you start dowsing amongst the choices, dowse and ask if there is an item on that list or in that row that is at least an 8 on a scale of 0-10, with 0 being poor and 10 being great. If you get 'no', then you may want to consider looking elsewhere, as we generally recommend 8 be the cutoff point for taking action.

If you are dowsing a written list of possible answers, always include 'Other' in the list, as you cannot know all the possible solutions. Point your finger at each item on the list, or say each item out loud, asking your dowsing question of each. Make a note of which ones test the best, then use dowsing to choose the best among those.

If 'Other' is chosen, then you have to go back and research some more and come up with other options. That can initially be a nuisance or a challenge, but in the long run, finding the best answer will save you time, effort and money.

Dive Deeper Into Dowsing In Our DVD Course

This book isn't intended to be a complete dowsing course. Our complete DVD course, Discovering Dowsing, will teach you everything you need to know to master dowsing. For details, visit http://discoveringdowsing.com/dowsing-course.

3

100 Ways To Use Dowsing

Warning!

Do not regard this book as some kind of bible. It is meant to be the first step in introducing you to the wonder and fun of dowsing. This book is designed to help you see how useful and fun dowsing can be in your life, but it can't cover all dowsing topics in depth. Check out our other books for more dowsing help. Our books may be bought at all major online retailers. Links to all stores may be found at Sixth Sense Books, http://sixthsensebooks.com/nonfiction-books.

If, like us, you find dowsing fascinating, we urge you to read our other books on dowsing, visit our website and learn as much as you can about it. It has totally changed our lives for the better, and we're pretty sure it can do the same for you.

Your success with dowsing will depend on your technique and how much you practice. We strongly urge you to take the time to visit our website Discovering Dowsing, as it will give you a firm foundation on dowsing technique.

Forming A Good Question

Why do you want a good dowsing question? Because the more specific the question is, the more helpful the answer will be. It takes a little practice, but it's worth it. So, we're going to share with you a basic step-by-step procedure that we use as a foundation for creating good dowsing questions. Our other books have more detailed information on dowsing technique, and we suggest you get them.

This book gives you 101 ways you can use dowsing that can change your life for the better. Included in each example is at least one good sample dowsing question on that topic. You can use the questions we provide, or you can refine them by customizing them using the procedure that follows.

Step 1: Think about your goals and make a list.

You need to include your goals in any question you ask. Everyone is unique, so it is useful to think carefully about why you want an answer to this dowsing question. Write the goals down. Be specific. Remember, specific=helpful!

Step 2: Include Who, What, Where, How, Why and When

Make notes of each of these as applicable for your question. Some things may not immediately be obvious, like 'when'. But they are all important. Some will be understood, like the 'who' often is you. But many people forget to add 'when' to their question and ask something like, "Am I deficient in vitamin C?". That is a poor question because it doesn't state a time frame. Adding 'at this time' makes it a better question.

A good example of how necessary a specific, detailed question is the story of the dowser doing a presentation in front of a group of people. He told them he could use his L-rod to show the direction of North. He said, "Show me North", and the L-rod kept pointing in a direction that was clearly NOT north. Finally, a man in the audience raised his hand and said, "It's pointing at me. My name is North." The presenter had not clearly defined his terms, and he got an answer that appeared wrong, but was actually right for the question he asked.

Using this type of exercise, finding how your question was right for what you asked, can help you improve your technique for making questions. And as you do, you'll see that good questions tend to be long and filled with detail.

Step 3: Word your question carefully to avoid anything vague. Terms like 'good', 'highest good' or 'best' are vague. Define clearly what it is you want to accomplish. Write the question down. Look at it critically and add whatever is needed.

Step 4: Get into a dowsing state and dowse the question.

Step 5: This last one is often overlooked. It's important that whenever possible, you verify your answers. That is the only way you will become confident. Writing the question down helps a lot, because you can go back and ask yourself how the answer you got, if it was wrong, could actually have been a right answer to the question you asked. Often, you will discover you left something out or didn't define a term clearly. Taking the time to do this will improve your technique immensely.

Programming Your Questions

What do you do in an emergency, and you want to use dowsing? Do you spend precious time carefully wording a long question? Of course not! What you do instead is have some pre-programmed dowsing questions at the ready.

Sounds strange? Maybe. But we like to program questions for emergencies. Things like whether it's necessary to take the cat to the vet with that injury. Or whether we need to see a doctor to resolve a problem we have. It's also quite useful to program questions when they are ones you use often at times when sitting and thinking about a question isn't easy to do.

The concept of programmed questions is slightly advanced, so if you can't get your head around it, feel free to skip this section. We will be referring to it in a few of the examples later in the book, and you can come back and read it if you wish.

When things are peaceful, follow the steps in the previous section for creating a good dowsing question, including writing it down. Next, decide what simple question you will want to use as the replacement for the long one you've written down. It will be a short one that's easy to remember.

Now, we're always saying don't use the word 'should' in a dowsing question, because it implies judgment, and generally we avoid doing that. But for our emergency question about taking a pet to the doctor, the simple question is, "Should we take_____(pet's name) to the vet?" That question replaces a much longer one that gives the conditions under which we would want a 'yes' answer or a 'no' answer, which might be hard to remember in an emergency. So we've programmed ourselves to ask the simple question, but it is understood to mean we want the answer to the longer one we programmed.

To program the question, you will need to get into a proper state for setting intention. It's like a dowsing state, but not quite. Some people term it an alpha brain state. In any case, clear your mind, empty it of thoughts, make sure you have no emotions active and then set your intention. Your intention is that when you ask the simple question ("Should I take Fluffy to the vet?"), you are really asking the dowsing question, "Given my goals and preferences and the knowledge and tools I possess at this time, is it preferable in terms of outcomes to take Fluffy to the vet for this injury?"

Before programming the question, you would have made a list of all the conditions that matter to you. They might include the upper limit of your finances or the fact that you have a lot of natural remedies and healing techniques you know that could help, and might even be faster or better than going to a vet. The question will also consider your values, such as you want to get a 'yes' for going to the vet if you don't have the tools at home to help Fluffy have a speedy recovery, or if she needs treatment you cannot give her.

Once you have set your intention to have the simple question represent the larger one, then anytime you dowse that simple question, it is understood that you want an answer to the longer, more detailed one.

Dowsing Ethics

Ethics is not taught in most dowsing courses. Certainly, we were not taught to think about dowsing ethics. One day a dear friend asked me to help her daughter, who was going through a very bad divorce. Her soon-to-be ex was a lawyer, and he was using his knowledge to slow the process and cost her money and prevent her from moving on. His latest trick was (yet again) not signing and returning a document on time, and this time, it was really going to cost her. My friend asked if I could help.

I told her if I got permission, I could see if I could shift the energy. You see, back then, as now, there was a lot of confusion about exactly what dowsing is, how it differs from intention and energy clearing techniques and what constitutes 'permission'. As I had been taught, I asked, "May I? Can I? Should I?" I got 'yes' to all. Then I asked if the ex's High Self was willing to give me permission to shift the energy to allow things to go smoothly and on time without conflict. I got another 'yes'. So I used intention to clear the energy that was blocking his acting in accord with the deadline. He signed the document right away, even though he lived in another state, never met me and had been dragging his feet consistently. Then within 24 hours, he went right back to being a real bastard.

What this taught me was that this is a free will Universe. He was as he was. He wanted to be that way. I may have gotten a slight change at a critical time, but it was not really what he would have chosen. My whole concept of permission changed. I realized that if the person would not agree if asked, that meant 'no'. I realized that to get real permission, I couldn't cheat by asking their High Self (which would usually say 'yes' to anything 'good'). And I also realized that using the "May I? Can I? Should I?" and dowsing for permission was circular-I was using dowsing to evaluate my dowsing. And since dowsing is not 100%, obviously my answers would not always be accurate.

Thus our dowsing evolved in a direction of thinking carefully about when it is appropriate to use dowsing, and when it is not. That is how we began to think about dowsing ethics. As we saw the many abuses (most of them well-intentioned) being perpetrated by dowsers (including ourselves), we realized that it was high time dowsing ethics was addressed in the dowsing community.

Don't get us wrong. We know that people who use dowsing have good intentions. But you know what they say about that. Good intentions are not enough. They do not take the place of using your head and being ethical. Just because you can dowse does not mean it's always appropriate to dowse.

Some of the biggest crimes we see in our society are from the attitude some people have that they should be allowed to exercise their power if they think it's a good thing. You probably wouldn't want someone tapping your phone or reading your email without permission. That's pretty obvious.

Even though almost every dowser would agree that reading someone's email without permission is unethical, some of those same people see nothing wrong with dowsing about other people without being asked to. They feel that because their intentions are good—they want to harmonize them or heal them or raise their frequency— that it is ok.

It isn't.

Sometimes in their hearts, they know it's wrong to dowse for or about another without being asked, so they say, "I asked their High Self/Spirit/the Universe for permission". Last time we looked, no one has a right to give you permission to read our email but us. That means, unless the person you want to dowse for or about asks you and says verbally that it's ok, DON'T DOWSE.

There are gurus who encourage what we would term unethical dowsing. Don't listen to them! Use your head and think through the ethics of what you intend. Don't just do something because someone says it's all right. That's like saying, "I was just following orders." And we don't have a lot of respect for that, do we?

Don't impose your idea of 'good' on other people. What you judge to be 'good' will not be agreeable to everyone. Raiding your mother's kitchen and throwing out all the junk food isn't going to change her health. It will make her angry. You wouldn't want someone to decide what's good for you and act on it unless you gave permission. You may have bad habits, but until you are ready to change them, you don't want anyone messing with you.

We are rabid about ethics, because unethical dowsing gives dowsing a bad name and makes people regard it as witchcraft. And there are indeed similarities between unethical dowsing and nasty voodoo or witchcraft that seeks to change or harm someone without permission.

Please take the time to ask for permission directly and respect the free will of others.

The 101 Amazing Ways To Use Dowsing

While this book lists over 101 ways you can use dowsing, the actual number is infinite. Our hope is that by giving you a glimpse at how versatile dowsing can be, you'll be encouraged to use it on a wider variety of subjects. We include questions for you to use, so you don't have to worry about making a good question. And we help give you ways to interpret your results.

We have ordered the examples from simple to more advanced. We urge you to go in order, though we know that not everyone will. It's simply too tempting to jump to the question you are eager to ask.

However, if you take the time to go through the examples in order, you will build your experience and your knowledge of dowsing as you go along, and your results will be more reliable. It's your choice!

4

Everyday Dowsing

1. The best vacation

Vacation time is precious. You probably will have a short list of places or concepts for your vacation. You may be traveling alone or with family or friends, and if you are traveling in a group, you will want to take everyone's preferences into account. You have limited resources to devote to vacation each year, and you can't afford to have it turn into a disaster. Yet we can all share stories of vacations that went badly wrong. Dowsing is a great way to make sure that never happens to you again.

Of course you are aware of the type of vacation you most like. But if you are traveling far from home or to new places, you cannot be sure that what you read or see online is accurate or will apply to you.

Make a list of your goals. Include weather, costs, activities, ambience and anything else that matters to you. Then take your top 3 choices and dowse.

Start with this one:

Considering my goals for my vacation in _____ *(name month and year) with* _____ *(list others if not traveling alone), are any of these places at least an 8 on a scale of 0-10 overall, with 0 being terrible and 10 being great?*

If you get 'yes', then test each one with this question:

How does _____ *(place/vacation package) rate on a scale of 0-10 overall for my goals for a great vacation in* _____ *(list month and year) with* _____ *(list traveling companions, if any)? 10? 9? 8? Etc.*

A score of 8 or higher is required for us to invest time and money. If you didn't get 'yes' to the first question, do some more research and make a new list of options. Obviously, go with a 10 if you can get it.

~

2. PICK A BIRTHDAY gift for your Mom

Have you ever spent hours shopping for the perfect gift for your Mom or boyfriend? Everywhere you go, you see nice things, but you just aren't sure. Nothing has 'hit' you as perfect, and your time and patience are running out.

Then while you are struggling to find a good gift, you remember last year when you bought those big, expensive Egyptian cotton towel sets in the perfect colors for your parent's master bathroom, to replace the thin, worn out ones they were using. They put the towels in a closet and never used them. It was kind of insulting after all the time and expense you went to. But what hurt most was you wanted them to have something nice they would love and use. And you felt like a failure.

Picking a gift for a loved one can be a real trial. You may not have a ton of money to spend, and you really want your gift to be special and loved. Or maybe you DO have a lot of money to invest, and you want to make sure it is a good investment.

Dowsing is so helpful when picking gifts. Often, it can be hard to guess what someone will love, unless they asked you for it. And, even if you think they'd like it, what if they already have one? Or what if they have a nicer one? We've all seen that gift recycling thing that happens to gifts that people don't want. You don't want your gift to end up at the holiday party giveaway at your friend's workplace because she doesn't want it.

Dowsing can dispel all the doubts you have when it's time to shop for a gift. We find it useful to use a series of questions for this purpose. The following questions start with finding out a type of gift, then drilling down and getting more specific. You don't have to use all these questions. You may already know some of the answers. Just use the questions for subjects you aren't sure about.

This question will only work with list dowsing or chart dowsing. So, make a list of types of items you would consider: clothing, a book, food, entertainment.

*What type of gift would _____(name person) most like for
_____(name event, like her next birthday) that costs
between_____(name the price range you are willing to spend)?*

Then point at or say each item on the list while asking the question, (spin your pendulum in a neutral swing or use deviceless dowsing) and wait for a 'yes', which will single out the best type. When you get a 'yes' for a category, like food, then you can drill down further. Making a chart is more effort, but a chart can be used as well.

Make a list of the food items you are considering: a bottle of wine, some fancy chocolates, a gift certificate to a restaurant. Dowse the list by asking the question as you point at or say each item. When you get a 'yes' with your pendulum or deviceless technique, then you have a specific gift.

*What type of food would_____(name person) most enjoy as a
_____(name event) gift?*

We like to use scales to make sure that the 'yes' is strong. You can either use this next question after choosing a particular item or incorporate the scale into the original question. So, for example, suppose you got a 'yes' for a gift certificate to a restaurant, you can then ask this question:

On a scale of 0 to 10, with 0 being no interest and 10 being total ecstasy, would a gift certificate to a restaurant rate 8 or higher in _____'s (name person) mind as a gift for _____(name event)?

This uses the scale dowsing discussed in an early chapter on how to dowse. It is very valuable to find a gift that ranks 8 or higher on this scale, as it makes it a sure thing for success.

As you go deeper into choosing the right gift, you will need to ask more questions. In this case, you'd want to find what type of restaurant or what particular restaurant your friend would consider an 8 or higher on a 0-10 scale for eating out. I

f you had gotten wine was the way to go, you'd need to dowse red or white, dry or sweet. Or you could dowse for a particular bottle right in the store. Here's a question you could use for picking a bottle of wine while in the store:

Is there any bottle of wine on this shelf that is a 10 on a scale of 0-10 for _____(name person) as a _____(name event) gift, and which costs no more than _____?

We would suggest going for a 10 if the selection is large, as obviously you want the best for the money. When you find the shelf where you get 'yes', then you can go along it, pointing at each bottle and using any deviceless technique to select the best one. Start by asking:

Give me a 'yes' when I am pointing at a bottle that is a 10 on the scale I just used.

Note how many are a 10. Then you can make a choice based on price, your past experience or what you think she'd like.

You can also use this for finding a wine for yourself!

3. FIND your lost keys (or other objects)

Most of us have lost our keys at some time or another. It can create a panic trying to find them, especially if they are the only set you have for your house or car. Discovering they are missing tends to happen when you are under pressure to use them quickly. You need to run out to the store or have an emergency, and while you scrounge around the house and garage looking for the keys, you are getting more stressed by the minute.

You last remember having them when you went grocery shopping two days ago. Obviously, you had to have them to get home, because the car and house keys are on the same ring. So you can logically assume they at least were in the car when you arrived home that day.

You'll need to ask a series of questions, because you can't be sure where they are at this time. If you park your car outside the house or live in an apartment, there's a slim chance you dropped them outside in a public area. If you own a house with a garage, probably the keys should be within the confines of your home and garage, unless someone in the family picked them up and put them somewhere.

Let's start by asking if they are currently inside the house or house and garage.

Is my key chain that I use when I go grocery shopping currently inside the house (house and garage)?

If you get 'yes', then you just have to search the premises. The questions to help with this are a little further down this section. If you get 'no', that means the keys are outside somewhere, or perhaps someone picked them up for you and has them off the property. If you got 'no', you can ask a variety of questions, such as:

Is that key chain I just asked about currently lying on the ground outside near the house, driveway or parking area?

Has someone found my key chain outside since I came home from the grocery store and picked it up and carried it somewhere?

Has someone turned my key chain in to the lost and found (if there is one) or management at this property?

Has someone found my key chain since I returned from the grocery store and taken it home, intending to turn it in, but has forgotten about it?

Has someone with criminal intentions stolen my key chain since I last went to the grocery store?

These are just a few possibilities. Remember to refer to the exact key chain you are missing (many folks have more than one). Refer to the time frame in which you lost it, or you might get an answer about another time you lost them.

If you got that the keys are inside your house/garage, you don't have to go room to room searching (but you can if you want). You could just sit at the kitchen table with a cup of coffee and ask:

Are the keys I usually take grocery shopping currently in my Ford Taurus?

Are the keys that I usually take grocery shopping currently in my brown purse?

Are the keys that I usually take grocery shopping currently in one of my coat pockets?

Are the keys that I usually take grocery shopping currently in_____(name a room)?

Dowsing is brilliant for finding lost objects, but the sad truth is that most people, even most experienced dowsers, are not experts at this subject. You see, there are so many applications in dowsing. And each person is drawn to one or a few of them.

We've observed that people tend to excel in certain types of dowsing, but not all applications. Just as most musicians play one or only a few instruments well, most dowsers have their specialties. If you become a good dowser of lost objects, you could make a lot of money, because there is a demand for that service.

∼

4. HIRE SOMEONE or do it myself?

We all like to save money. But it can be a pain to do-it-yourself, and often, you don't have the right tools or the ability to do a great job. So, when it's unclear whether it's wiser to hire a specialist or do-it-yourself, dowsing comes to the rescue.

Dowsing will help you decide the best choice, and if you would be better off hiring someone, dowsing can help you choose the best person for the job.

Consider the project you need to complete. What are your goals? What are your priorities? Everyone is different. Do you have the budget in mind as your highest priority? Do you want to spend less than X dollars on the project? Do you fear that hiring a professional will bust the budget? On the other hand, you might not be as concerned about money, though it is a factor. You are more concerned about doing the job well and having it be high quality and lasting. Or perhaps you are aware that you lack talents in the DIY field, and you don't have a lot of tools, so you are aware that a professional might be your best bet, but you still are not sure.

Take time consider your goals in this project. What are your priorities? Then dowse the following question:

Considering my goals and priorities for the completion of this project, is hiring a professional preferable to doing the project myself?

If you get yes, then you need to choose a professional. We've found it useful to use the Yellow Pages or any other listing of professional services as a dowsing resource. We focus on our goals and then dowse the list of people who are offering the services we need:

Is anyone in this list an 8 or better on a scale of 10 for completing my project based on my goals and priorities, with 0 being poor and 10 being great?

If the answer is yes, then list dowse to find out the ones who are 8 or better. Then find out the best one, by asking if anyone is a 10, a 9, etc.

If when you dowse the first question, you get no, that doing it yourself is better, then go with that.

~

5. THE BEST **dinner menu**

Having a dinner party or event where you have to feed guests? Dowsing is a great way to insure your success. These days, people are more aware of food allergies and have preferences that are pretty unusual compared to the past. And often, they won't want to put you out by telling you what their preferences are.

Maybe they follow the Paleo diet and don't eat grains, which are pervasive in our culture. Perhaps they have dairy or nightshade allergies and don't want to mention them. Dowsing will help you choose a menu that will be perfect for everyone. Of course, the more people you invite, the more challenging it becomes, but dowsing can insure success.

Like we've said before, make a list of your goals. It will depend on what lengths you are willing to go to and what expense you will accept for success. Maybe some of your guests only eat organic. Others have food allergies. Decide how much you want to accommodate your guests. Maybe you want to make sure no one gets an allergic reaction or digestive upset. Perhaps you want to take it one step further and make sure everyone finds the food tasty and delicious as well as nutritious.

Once you have decided on your goals regarding your guests and their satisfaction, make a list of choices for appetizers, main courses, etc. Then use dowsing to pick the best choices for your needs. Here's a question you can use:

Considering my priorities and goals for my dinner party/event, which of the following is the best choice for _____(appetizer, main course, etc) for my dinner party guests on _____(name the date of your event)?

This is a list dowsing question. See the earlier chapter for how to list dowse. Make sure any list contains 'other' as a choice, because you might not have anything in mind that will work well.

A better question altogether is using scales:

Considering my goals for my dinner party guests on _____(name the date), are any of these choices an 8 or better on a scale of 10, with 0 being no good for my goals and 10 being perfect?

If you can't get any good choices, then go back to the drawing board and come up with some other options and re-dowse them. If you still can't get any winners (8 or higher on a scale of 10), then maybe you need to lower your expectations and loosen up your restrictions. Maybe you are asking for too much in terms of success given the number of people and their particular needs. Use your judgment, but be willing to lower your standards a little bit if needed.

~

6. THE BEST makeup

I have an allergy to some ingredient in mascara. In fact, I find that most eye makeup irritates my eyes. I'm so grateful I don't have to wear makeup every day. On the rare occasions that I have had to wear makeup for a whole day, I often found that the next day, my eyes were red and irritated.

I know that artificial ingredients and chemicals can be harmful. And the skin can absorb noxious ingredients. So it's important to choose makeup and personal care products like skin lotions and shampoos with care. I finally made a commitment to do a little research so I could find a mascara that wouldn't give me an allergic reaction. I had never found any of the drug store brands tolerable, even those labeled 'hypoallergenic'. Even when I used a better brand of makeup, I still had problems. So I made an investment in a very expensive mascara I found after researching on the internet, hoping it would be great. It claimed to be perfect for people like me.

I used it with great expectations, but I got the same reaction I always do. And it was disappointing, considering the amount of money I'd invested. Why hadn't I bothered to dowse? The rational mind can only do so much research. And the rational mind cannot sort the claims made by manufacturers. But dowsing can show you whether the claims will work in your case.

So if you would like to find a line of makeup or hair care product or skin care products that are truly hypoallergenic for you and meet your other requirements, dowsing is going to save you. First, make a list of your goals. Maybe you want makeup that lasts all day, is made from natural ingredients and won't give you any allergic reaction.

Next, do your research. Perhaps you will talk to friends who have lots of experience using various brands of makeup. Or you can do an internet search. Once you have a short list of possible brands, you then need to dowse before investing in anything. Use this question:

Considering all my goals, is _____(brand) of_____(product, such as mascara) an 8 or higher on a scale of 10 overall, with 10 being perfect?

Then of course you have to buy and use it and see what happens. In any case, I bet you get better results than I did, since I forgot to dowse!

∼

7. FIND underground cables and pipes

One day, there was a knock on our door. A neighbor was standing there. Previously, he had told us he liked us, even though he thought we were a bit weird. But now he was looking a bit sheepish. He was building a garage for his RV, and he needed to find the buried water lines on his property so he would not cut through them. He knew we were dowsers, and he thought maybe we could help him. And we did. Finding things that are buried is not easy. But dowsing gives you radar vision in that regard.

We went to his house and showed him how to dowse and let him find where the water lines were. He was thrilled. He went into the house and told his wife he had learned how to dowse. He was a retired Math professor, and it was a real treat to see him discover the power of dowsing. He went on to complete his project with no damage to buried services.

Do you need to dig on your property, but you aren't quite sure where the water, gas or other lines are buried? Maybe you need to find the exact location of your septic tank so it can be pumped. We once used dowsing for that with terrific results.

Dowsing can help you avoid cutting through buried services when you dig. Either you will be trying to find the location of underground objects, or you will be trying to avoid them. Either way, the dowsing is much the same. Let's start with how you dowse to locate the septic tank or any underground services.

We suggest using L-rods when working outdoors, because they are less affected by wind and the movement of your body while you walk. You can see videos on how to use L-rods at our website, http://discoveringdowsing.com.

Go to the area you wish to survey for the particular underground service, in this example, the lid to your septic tank that is the one that needs to be accessed so it can be pumped out.

You will want to walk a grid pattern of the area, focusing on your question and asking to get a yes response when you cross over the top of the septic tank that you are seeking. You can be very specific and ask that you get a 'yes' when your leading food crosses over the near edge of the lid of the tank.

Please give me a 'yes' response when my leading foot crosses over the near edge of the lid of the septic tank that I need to remove in order to have the tank pumped.

A lid is roughly circular, so you can continue to dowse and sketch out the dimensions of the lid. We have a photo we took of the hole we dug after dowsing the lid to our septic tank. It was exactly the size of the lid.

You can adapt this to water or gas lines or electrical cables by changing the wording slightly.

Give me a 'yes' response when my leading foot crosses over the _____(cable, water line, gas line).

You can also use dowsing to track the path of the cable or line from your house to the edge of your property. In that case, once you locate the cable or pipe, you can use one L-rod to indicate the direction it goes in. As you walk, just ask to be shown where the pipe or cable goes. The L-rod will appear to lead you along the path of the pipe or cable. This is a different use of the L-rod from asking a yes/no question.

∼

8. Where to find an item

Do you love to shop or hate to shop? Either way, dowsing can make shopping more fun. Most people don't actually like dragging through store after store looking for an item at the right price. They would rather go straight to the store that has it at the best price and get done with it. Both Nigel and I are like that. We just prefer to get it done quickly. Dowsing can help you do that, saving you time and effort, and even saving you money. Because if you don't check out all the sources, you might pay more than you have to for your item.

Think about your priorities and goals for buying this particular item. Are you looking for the best price? A certain color? A maintenance agreement that is super? Be sure to add if you need it to be in stock at this time. Once you are clear on your goals, make a list of stores that you believe will have the item. Add 'other' to the list. Then list dowse (ask the same question for every store on the list) using the following question:

Which of these stores is the best place for me to achieve my goals in wanting to buy _____(name the item) within_____(name the time frame)?

If you get 'other', you need to research other places where you could buy the object. Always check your results and see how happy you feel with them. Remember, dowsing is not 100% accurate, even for the best dowsers. The point is that it is better than trial and error, which is the only other alternative.

And, just as some people can be really brilliant at finding lost objects, it could turn out that one of your great dowsing skills is locating which place to go… You won't know until you try!

9. DOES my car need work?

Cars. They're kind of like computers. Can't live with them, can't shoot them.

Unless you're one of the rare types who is good at car repair, you dread being told that your car needs expensive work done to it. Yet how often has that happened? I remember one time when I was in college, I owned a 10-yr-old Volkswagen Beetle. It was my first car. It had three dented fenders and was very basic, being a 1965 model. And it seemed that something was always going wrong with it.

I bought a book that had a title like "The Guide To Repairing Your VW Beetle For The Complete Idiot." It guided me through oil changes, rebuilding the carburetor, adjusting the gaps on the spark plugs and a variety of other jobs that saved me money. But one day I was getting gas, and the attendant told me that my car needed work. He pointed to fluid leaks on the ground near my wheels and said I needed new shocks. It was a very costly job, but I was afraid not to have it done. Later I found that he was running a common scam played on unsuspecting motorists, usually women.

If I had been a dowser then, I could have used dowsing to find out how true it was that my car needed new shocks. I can't recover the money lost that time, but I have never had to worry about being lied to by a mechanic since I became a confident dowser.

Rather than asking if the mechanic is telling you the truth when he says you need a brake job or a head gasket, dowse on a scale of 0-10 using the following question. (*Bear in mind that the goals are assumed to be that you have your car in good working order, safe working order and repair or replace anything in a timely fashion that would threaten those goals.*)

Considering the goals I have for the safe and reliable function of my car, how valuable would it be at this time to _____ (name the suggested repair).

If the job is critical and failing to do it will make the car unreliable or unsafe, you will get an 8 or higher for doing the job at this time. Less than a 3 means it really isn't needed badly at this time. 4-7 means it is approaching needing it. You could dowse further if the number is between 4 and 7, and find out if, even though it isn't critical yet, now might be a good time to repair or replace the part to avoid a breakdown or greater expense in the future. We suggest that unless the number is 8 or higher, you get a second opinion before having any work done.

∾

10. The best restaurant

If you need to choose a restaurant to hold a party, like for a wedding anniversary, there are a number of factors you want to consider. Do they have a special room of the right size for your party? What type of food do they serve? Is it really good? Will it please the majority of your guests? Is it conveniently located for most of your guests?

You can do a lot of thinking logically and narrow your list down to a few choices you feel might be good. But if one doesn't jump out at you, dowsing can come to the rescue. Assuming you've carefully thought out what your priorities are, so you can be sure to dowse the best restaurant, use the following question for each of the 'finalist' restaurants:

How does _____(name the restaurant) rank on a scale of 0-10, with 0 being terrible and 10 being perfect as the venue for _____(name your event) on_____(name your date or date range)? 0? 1? 2? 3? (Keep asking until you get 'yes').

If none of them rank 8 or higher, consider looking for other options. 8 is the lowest number we would consider for anything requiring an investment of money.

∼

11. Which menu item?

When you eat out, on special occasions or if you rarely get to eat out, you want to really enjoy your meal. That may be why so often, people will choose the same meal every time they go somewhere, because at least they can be sure that one will please them. It's so disappointing paying for a meal and not enjoying it.

Dowsing is perfect for scouting the menu in a restaurant for the first time, or going beyond your tried and true menu item. As always, consider what your goals and priorities are. Does it matter to you whether there are allergens in the food? Do you have touchy digestion and want something that won't give you a bad reaction? Do you hate garlic, but you're just not sure the waitress will know if there is garlic in that item?

Think about your goals. You want the meal to be enjoyable. Add any other priority you have.

If you've never eaten at this restaurant, then you might want to start out by asking:

Is there at least one item among the main courses/appetizers/desserts listed on this menu that is 8 or higher on a scale of 0 to 10, with 0 being terrible and 10 being terrific for my goals and priorities at this time?

If you get 'no', then you might want to go to another restaurant.

If you get 'yes' (or if you skip that question, because you know the place has great food), then use list dowsing to find the page and column that the best item is on, then list dowse and find the one that meets your criteria. List dowsing technique is covered in an earlier section of this book. Assuming that you trust the quality of this restaurant to offer you at least one item that is 8 or better on a scale of 0-10, with 0 being terrible and 10 being terrific, you can dowse this question:

Is the menu item (or main course/appetizer/dessert) that I would enjoy most, considering all my priorities, on this page/in this column?

Then dowse each item in that smaller list, pointing your finger at each selection.

Is this the main course/appetizer/dessert I would most enjoy based on my priorities and goals tonight?

In situations like this, one of your biggest challenges will be to follow what your dowsing says. What if your dowsing indicates that you should choose the chicken, and you prefer beef? Choose the chicken and expect good results. If you don't trust your dowsing, you'll never improve. And it's really cool when dowsing opens new doors to unexpected fun.

~

12. Pick the best movie

Dowsing is quite useful for making the most of your entertainment time. Nothing is more disappointing than picking a rotten movie to watch in your precious free time. You can use this same question for any type of entertainment, like a novel or an event.

Consider what your goals are. Some days you just want escapist fun. Other days you might like some mental stimulation. Maybe you just want to feel entertained and enjoy watching something without bothering too much about who's in it or the type of movie. So be very clear about what you want the movie to do for you. Also, if you are planning on watching it with someone else, consider what their goals and preferences are.

Dowsing for just your own preferences will often come up with different answers than dowsing for a group of friends or family with varying interests.

This is a good basic question:

Considering my goals (or the preferences and goals of the group), how would this movie rate on a scale of 0 to 10 for watching tonight (or give another time), with 0 being awful and 10 being amazing?

As always, go with your answer and see what happens. It's the best way to build your confidence in your dowsing.

~

13. Which music CD?

Maybe you like music, but you have a lot of choices of what to listen to. You may need to select some CDs for a car trip you are taking. Or maybe you just want to chill out and listen to some music tonight, but you're not really sure what would be most pleasing.

Dowsing is a great way to pick music that will be just the right thing for you at any given time. Reflect on your mood, your preferences and your goals for listening to music, and then dowse this question:

Which of these CDs will be the best choice for me to listen to now/for the next _____minutes/on my trip to Sedona, considering my preferences and goals at this time?

Point at each CD and ask to get a 'yes' response when you are pointing at one that is best. If you are looking for more than one CD, include that in the question, noting how many you want to choose overall, then ask as you point at each CD if that is one of the best.

∼

14. The best parking space

Finding a good parking space at Costco on a cold or rainy day can be a challenge. You don't want to have to walk far, and maybe you wish to be close to the cart corral. You can't possibly see where the best open space is, and as busy as traffic is in the lot, even if you see one, it may be taken by the time you get to it.

Dowsing is a great way to find a good parking space in a crowded lot. We use it all the time, and our results are over 90% satisfying. Much better than just guessing or fishing around.

But how do you do that? You're driving and paying attention to the traffic. The first thing to say is only use deviceless dowsing when driving. It's much safer and easier. Holding a pendulum and driving just doesn't cut it! Blink dowsing is our favorite technique, and you can see how to do that at our website, http://discoveringdowsing.com by entering 'blink dowsing' in the Search box on any page but the Home page.

This dowsing question is based on our desire to find a legal space as close to the entrance as possible that will be the right size and available when we get our car to it. We ask which lane to turn down to get to that space, which involves asking several times until we find the space.

Because driving takes all your attention, this is a good question to program. See the section on programming earlier in the book for details.

The simple question we ask is,

Which way do I turn to find the best parking space? (Look or point left and then right, waiting for the 'yes' response).

When you get an answer, turn in that direction and ask the question again at the next choice of turnings. Keep asking until you find the space. Then note if it appears to be the best one.

Please note that this is a programmed question, and it will not give you good results unless you take the time to formulate a longer, more specific question that includes all of your desired factors and then program it.

Our longer question is something like, "Considering that I want the closest legal parking space that is empty at this time and will remain empty until I reach it, and that is the right size for my car and closest to the entrance, which direction do I turn to find it?" You can see how having a simple question you use instead is much easier than trying to remember the long question.

15. Which jacket?

Depending on where you live, dressing for the weather can be challenging at times. Here is Arizona, we rarely carry a rain jacket, even when the skies are gray, because rain is so rare. But back in Virginia, any morning that looked threatening meant having to decide about carrying an umbrella and raincoat to work. And often, it isn't convenient to carry things around when you aren't going to need them.

In transitional seasons like spring and fall, you can be either overdressed or underdressed badly for the weather, as it can be changeable in many places. I can remember going out one late fall day in pleasant weather wearing a sweater and no jacket and returning in a blizzard, having to abandon my car about a mile from home. The walk was not pleasant…Dowsing is a great way to avoid this kind of discomfort and inconvenience.

Think about your concerns about the weather at this time. You might sum them up by saying you want to wear or carry the best clothing and accessories to accommodate the weather you will be out in over the course of the coming 12 hours. If you work indoors, you may only face the weather on the way to work, at lunchtime and on the way home. If you work outdoors, you are concerned about what to wear for your comfort and safety for the whole day. Think about your goals and priorities.

Then dowse this question and point at the jackets and coats in your closet as if you are list dowsing:

Considering my goals for comfort, health and safety, give me a 'yes' when I point at the best topcoat/jacket to wear with this outfit today to best care for me when I am exposed to the weather.

You can also dowse about carrying an umbrella, boots or other accessories. In those cases, it usually is not a choice among many, but rather is a simple yes/no.

Considering the weather for the rest of today and my goals for safety, comfort and health, will it be significantly advantageous for me to wear boots/carry an umbrella/ wear a hat in addition to my other outerwear?

If you get a perplexing answer, you could be wrong, or maybe you are right, and like me and the blizzard, you are going to have an unexpected exposure to weather that day. Trust your dowsing. On questions like this, a wrong answer isn't life or death, and it will build your confidence.

16. Which beer?

We've all been to one of those restaurants or grills where they have 100 different brands of beer. Or maybe it just seems that way, they have so many choices. Dowsing is a great way to pick the perfect beer from among a bunch of brands you don't know.

Consider your goals. Are you just having a beer with some nuts or chips? Or are you going to have a meal? What is the meal? Once you are clear what your goals are, then list dowse the options using this question:

Considering my goals for having this beer, which choice will be most pleasing to me as a beverage to have with _____(name the meal or snack) at this time?

You can run your finger down a list on the menu, asking for a 'yes' when you point at the best selection. Or you can let your gaze scan from left to right along a row of bottles, asking for the 'yes' when you are looking directly at the best choice for the above question.

It's always wise to double check answers when list dowsing, because you might actually have meant the item just before or after the one you were pointing at was best. So double check by asking about the items on either side of the one you believe gave you the 'yes' answer, just for good measure.

17. What's the best hotel?

So you've decided to go to Cancun. But you've never been there before, and there are so many choices for hotels, or even vacation rentals, that you are overwhelmed. Here's a perfect way to use dowsing to get better results!

Make a list of your goals. Do you want a kitchen? Where exactly do you want to be located? Do you want waterfront? A pool?

When your list is complete, do your due diligence and research some of the options. Visit whatever website you like to use to see reviews of places for vacationers. This is the left brain part of your dowsing activity. Your rational mind can narrow the field quite a bit, but you will be left with a few to several places to choose from, all of them attractive and meeting most, if not all, of your requirements.

Now get a rating for each of those places on a scale of 0-10:

Considering all of my goals, what is the rating overall on a scale of 0 to 10, with 10 being the best, for _____(name the hotel or vacation rental property) for my vacation to Cancun in May of next year?

We recommend that you do not invest in anything that tests lower than 8. Preferably, you want a 10. Pick the one that ranks highest among those you dowsed. If none is an 8, go back and search some more.

If you have two that are tied, you can make a separate list of your goals and test each place on each goal.

On a scale of 0 to 10, with 10 being best, how does _____(name the hotel or vacation rental) test for _____(name the goal) for my vacation to Cancun in May of next year?

The first question gave you an average for all your goals. Testing each goal separately will show you the strengths and weaknesses of each property and allow you to make a better choice. For example, you might test separately for subjects like, safety, convenience to restaurants, closeness to a good snorkeling beach, reliable wifi, etc.

~

18. Will I run out of gas?

You know you shouldn't have waited so long, but still, it happened. Your gas gauge is on Empty. You're not sure how much gas is left, but you're running on fumes.

There's a gas station coming up, but the prices are steep, because it's close to the interstate. Or maybe you don't like it because it sells cheap gas that is dirty and gives your car trouble. Either way, you'd rather not buy gas there unless you have to. You want to wait for the next station, which is 10 miles away. You're not sure you'll make it that far. What to do?

You cannot know the answer by using your rational mind. But you can find out the answer through dowsing. This is an excellent situation to use your blink dowsing (see the section on tools earlier in this book), as you are driving and want to keep your hands on the wheel. Even if you pull over to dowse, it will be easiest to use a deviceless technique.

If I do not get gas at this station here, will the car run out of gas before I reach the _____(name to brand of the next station) station down this road (or you can say, 'the next gas station on this road')?

If you get 'yes', stop and get some gas here. But make a note of how much you bought and try to see if you think you would have made it. If you get 'no', and you're feeling brave, go with your dowsing and see what happens.

∾

19. Will Dad like this gift?

It's frustrating to buy a special gift, only to discover the recipient already has one. Or maybe, you thought it was a good idea, but it gets put on a shelf and never used. Most of us have experienced this with close friends and family. With dowsing, you never have to go through that again.

As always, do your research and pick what you think is the best gift you can imagine. Once you have an item in mind, dowse the following questions:

If I buy this _____*(name the gift) for*_____*(the recipient) for his/her*_____*(the event) this year, how much will he/she like it on a scale of 0 to 10, with 10 being a lot? 10? 9? 8? Etc.*

*If I buy this*_____*(name the gift) for* _____*(the recipient) for his/her*_____*(the event) this year, will he/she use it?*

*Does*_____*(name the person) already have a*_____*(name the item specifically)?*

You'll find your dowsing improves faster if you keep a journal of your dowsing questions and answers on subjects like these and go back and make a note of how things turned out. If the results were not good, look hard at your dowsing answer and see how it could be correct for the question you asked. If the question is vague or incomplete, the answer may be incorrect or useless. This will teach you how to make good dowsing questions and improve your accuracy.

~

20. Which library book?

This will work for either choosing a book online from the library or choosing one from a shelf in the library in person. Go about narrowing the search as you usually do. You know what you're in the mood for. Maybe you want a biography. Or a mystery. Go to the appropriate section and start browsing.

You can ask about all the books on one shelf or in one column in the listing online.

Considering my preferences, are any of the books on this shelf/in this column an 8 or higher on a scale of 0 to 10 for my personal enjoyment this weekend (or whatever time frame), with 10 being best?

If you want, you can ask for a 10. When you get a 'yes', then you can point with your finger and scan the row or column, asking:

Please give me a 'yes' response when my finger is pointing at any book in this row/column that is at least an 8 on a scale of 0 to 10 for my preferences.

Then check the book out and read it to see how your dowsing was.

~

21. Get the warranty?

Extended warranties. They're a nuisance. It's hard to decide whether to get them or not. Most of the time, we say no to them. However, if you are buying an expensive item, like a computer, maybe you feel it could be worth considering protecting your investment.

Dowsing will help you decide whether you need to purchase that extended warranty, saving you a ton of money over the years. Because each person is unique, you need to consider your priorities before dowsing. Is money tight? Would you like to make that your big priority, not to spend money you don't need to? Or are you concerned about whether the warranty is going to be worth the money you invest? How can you be sure what might or might not go wrong with your item? And the warranty may not cover everything.

So the idea is to get some guidelines. You don't want to invest in a warranty if this item isn't going to break down, or if future breakdowns are likely not to be covered by the warranty, or if any breakdown would be cheaper to cover on your own. So dowse the following after you are clear about your priorities.

Considering my goals and priorities, will it be worthwhile for me to purchase the extended warranty for _____(name the price or time frame or both) for this item?

As always, go with your dowsing and see the results. If you are
fortunate enough to plan ahead or have a dowsing buddy with you at
the time, get a second opinion before making a purchase.

~

22. Choose the best route

You have a number of ways you can get to work, but sometimes,
depending on traffic or accidents, you can get stuck. There may be no
way to predict which route is fastest on any given day. But dowsing
will allow you to pick the best route. Ask this question about each
route, giving it a clear name that differentiates it from other routes you
could choose.

*Defining 'best' as safest and quickest, is _____(name the route)
the best way for me to get to work this morning among the choices I have?*

This is one of those dowsing exercises that you won't usually be able to
confirm accuracy on, unless you later hear about an accident or road
work on a route you avoided thanks to dowsing. But it can really
reduce your stress when your commute is smoother, and this is a
technique we often use when faced with a number of similar routes to
a particular destination.

~

23. Where's the leak?

It can be very frustrating to find the source of a leak in your irrigation
system or plumbing. There are pitfalls in dowsing for this that you
can't imagine. I can remember dowsing for leaks in my irrigation
system very early in my dowsing career. I got that yes, there was
a leak.

I dowsed where the leak was. I was taken to a tree. I marked the spot
and dug and dug. The part of the irrigation system that I revealed sat

there slowly dripping. Drip, drip, drip. Indeed, there was a 'leak', but it wasn't anything serious. I had not thought to define the term carefully before dowsing. So I was led on a merry chase that turned out to be nothing.

There are many symptoms that can cause you to suspect a leak. Maybe you have the obvious one of water pouring down through the ceiling in your living room (been there, done that). Or perhaps you get a suspiciously high water bill and see that your water usage is off the charts. That might indicate a leak in your irrigation or plumbing. But if you haven't seen water, how do you find the leak or even confirm it exists?

This is a pretty tricky situation, and dowsing can save you a lot of time and trouble, even money. First, you need to determine if you have a leak. Then, you need to find the source. It all comes down to asking the right question.

The first question you need to ask is if you have a significant leak. It is not uncommon to have slight leakage at joints and such, and you don't want to count that, unless the leak is so bad that you are losing a lot of water. Think carefully about what 'significant' means to you in this situation. Then start with this question:

If I define 'leak' as a significant loss of water from my plumbing/irrigation system, do I have one or more leaks in my system?

If you get 'yes', then an L-rod (or 2) are the best way of locating the actual leak itself. If you aren't sure how to use L-rods (and only one is needed), visit our Discovering Dowsing website and watch the video on the use of this tool. The L-rod is particularly useful outdoors when walking around, even when wind is present. It doesn't react as much as a pendulum will, and it has the benefit of pointing out direction.

This exercise is more complex than many others in this book. You will need to find the location of the water pipes or irrigation lines using your L-rod, and then walk along those lines asking the following question:

Please show me a 'yes' response when I walk over the location of a significant leak in this water system.

So you can see you'll first need to chart where the pipes or water lines run. Then walk along them, asking to get a 'yes' response where any significant leak is. Then dig down to see if you are correct.

The same procedure can be followed for water lines inside and under the house. However, it's obvious that digging will not be an easy option in this case. You will need to resort to hiring a professional once you have located the leak.

~

24. Find where a cable runs in the wall

A stud finder seemed a miraculous device to me when I was first introduced to it. It 'saw' into walls, revealing where the studs were, so that I could drive a nail into a stud if hanging an item on the wall. Dowsing has the same magical appeal, showing you where the objects you seek run behind the wall.

You can use an L-rod or pendulum and walk along a wall, pointing a finger at it, asking to get a 'yes' response when you cross the cable or whatever you are seeking. It is useful to scan the wall in the horizontal and then the vertical directions to pinpoint what you are looking for.

Please give me a 'yes' response when my finger crosses over the electrical cable (or whatever you are seeking) that is running behind this wall.

Though no one likes making holes in walls, this is a pretty easy thing to confirm about your dowsing. We found this technique to be useful when we were putting dog doors into the walls of two different houses we lived in. We wanted to avoid electrical cables and studs, and dowsing helped us to do that. Nothing like putting a hole in a wall to find out you are in a bad place. Dowsing saved the day for us, and we think it can help your DIY projects, too.

25. Choose a plumber

Choosing a professional of any type can be a challenge. You want someone who will do a good job for the best price. Someone knowledgeable. Make a list of the things that matter to you. Do you care about guarantees? Price? Honesty? Qualifications to handle the job? Someone who shows up on time and completes the job in a timely fashion?

Once you have your goals in mind, you can go to the yellow pages or any other list for the type of provider you are looking for.

On a scale of 0 to 10, with 10 being best, are any of the professionals listed in this category an 8 or above overall for the goals I have for this project?

If no one is 8 or higher, look elsewhere. If anyone is 8 or higher, then separate them by rank. Go for a 10 if possible. Then make an appointment and see what happens. It doesn't hurt to screen the person before making an appointment by letting them know what your project is and what your goals are. Sometimes you have a surprising outcome.

When we were looking for someone to replace some defective windows, we wanted to find the guy who had done the job a few years earlier, but we couldn't find his card, and we couldn't remember his name. Nothing in the yellow pages looked familiar.

The company that dowsed best for our needs was mainly aimed at contractors. It didn't make sense to call them, but I did. When I told them what I wanted, they told me they refer that work to a guy, and they gave me his contact information. Turned out to be the guy I was looking for…

26. Finding the lid for the septic tank

Dowsing for underground stuff can be kind of exciting. Once you start digging, you get confirmation about whether you were right or wrong. Years ago, we were going to have our septic tank pumped. The company told us we'd save $50 if we dug the hole ourselves, and at that time, that was a lot of money to us. So we went out in the general area we knew the tank was, and we dowsed where to find the top of it. Nigel found one location, and I found another, not several inches away.

We dug down and discovered that there were two handles on the lid at the top of the tank, one at the location he had found, and one at the location I had marked. The hole we dug was exactly the width of the top. The guy who came to pump the tank was quite impressed. We took a picture to commemorate it. We don't do a lot of underground dowsing, so it was cool to see how well it worked.

You might want to use a question like this in this situation:

Considering I want to find the exact location of the top of my septic tank that will allow the system to be pumped, please give me a yes when I cross over an edge of that top with my left foot.

Mark the location of the 'yes' response. It will be a circle or roughly that. Then dig. Good luck!

∿

27. How's my roof?

Replacing your roof is a hugely expensive proposition. So you don't want to do it when you don't have to. But you don't want to wait too late. If you do, you could have all kinds of problems. So it's a good idea to check the condition of your roof from time to time and plan to take action to replace it when needed.

You can evaluate the condition of your roof on a scale of 0 to 10, with 10 being best. You can define what number you feel would mean it's time to replace or repair the roof. You might say that you want to know what number indicates that there will be damage like rain damage or wind damage or other problems due to age and weathering.

For us, an 8 or higher is usually a good number. A 3 or lower is usually a bad number in this case. Numbers in between are transitional and may or may not indicate a need to take action. It depends on how you define things.

In any case, it is ideal to get an 8 or higher on a scale of 10. If you get that, you're fine. Anything less, you might want to dowse further and see if action is appropriate.

Considering all the factors that contribute to integrity and function, what is the rating of my roof on a scale of 0 to 10, with 10 being excellent?

Of course this same process can be used to evaluate other key parts of your home, like the furnace, air conditioner or water pump for your well.

28. Need chimney cleaning?

Do you have a chimney, and do you clean it every year? We don't use our fireplace a lot. Not even every day. So we don't feel we need to professionally clean our chimney every year. It will depend on your usage and what kind of wood you are burning. Dowsing will help you decide when you need to hire a chimney sweep.

You want to take into account safety issues and the efficient function of your fireplace and chimney. You can check the overall function of the fireplace and chimney. That might be separate from the need for a sweep. In this case, our question purely relates to the appropriateness of hiring a chimney sweep to clean your chimney.

On a scale of 0 to 10, with 10 being absolutely necessary, what is the advantage to the overall safe and efficient function of my fireplace of hiring a chimney sweep to clean my chimney? 10? 9? 8?

8 or higher means make an appointment with a chimney sweep.

29. Which decorator?

Word of mouth is the best way to find a good service provider. But what if you are new to an area and have no friends to consult? Or for some other reason don't have someone to consult? That's when dowsing is your best friend.

We've all scanned the yellow pages from time to time, trying to find a good plumber or electrician or whatever. But even after reading the ads, it seems hard to decide. In the past, you've guessed wrong as often as you've guessed right. And that can be a costly mistake.

For something like an interior decorator, which usually is a big job, you don't want to make mistakes. This same technique will work for hiring a contractor for building your new home.

Dowsing won't let you down when done properly. Of course you need to have good dowsing technique and ask a great question, but those are easy to learn. So let's assume you are a good dowser. Where do you begin on this subject?

Make a written list of what matters most to you in choosing this decorator. Be detailed and specific. Take time on this step, because it is very important. Your dowsing can only guide you to what you are asking for, so you need to ask well.

Some of the things that may matter include:

- Quality of workmanship
- Pricing
- Guarantees
- Ability to do your job in a certain time frame
- Good communication
- Has the same tastes as you

- Willingness to accept credit cards

Your list might include other things, things that are specific to your task. Be sure to include them all. Then dowse using a scale of 0 to 10 to find the best provider.

Considering all the goals on my list and the priorities I give them, is anyone listed in this section of the yellow pages an 8 or better on a scale of 10 for satisfying my goals?

If you get 'yes', you can ask which ones are 8 or better. Point at each listing and ask:

Is this one an 8 or better?

Make a list with all the finalists, then dowse which one is best overall for your goals. Call and make an appointment.

30. How useful is this product?

Advertising can be deceptive. Dowsing can help you determine how accurate an advertised product or service is for your particular needs. No product or service is perfect for everyone. Wouldn't it be great to be sure you were investing your money wisely, and that you would get the results the ad promises?

In this case, make a list of the claims in the ad that matter to you. Then dowse using a simple question like this:

Will _____(name the product advertised) provide me with all the claims made in that ad?

You could ask in other ways:

On a scale of 0 to 10, with 0 being not at all, how likely is it that if I buy and use that product, I will get the results promised in that ad? 10? 9? 8? Etc.

If I buy that product, will I be satisfied with the results I get?

You can be as specific as you like, and the more specific you get, the more likely your answer will be meaningful and useful.

31. Is this estimate true?

When money is tight (and even when it is not), an unexpected repair bill can be traumatic. We've all had the major car repair, furnace replacement or roof leaking situation to face. But what's even worse than an unexpected large expense is wondering if someone is being honest with you. Or maybe you wonder if they have padded the estimate.

Many of us have been fooled on occasion in the past about the need for a particular home repair. We said yes when we should have said no. We were ignorant and trusted the 'expert' to be honest, but he wasn't.

There's always the chance that someone will try to take advantage of your ignorance or situation and tell you that you need a repair or replacement that you don't really need. Dowsing is a great way to protect yourself when you can't rationally know if someone is telling the truth or not, and you really need to make the right choice.

This is a situation that you could approach in a variety of ways in terms of questions. As always, the more specific you are, the better. Here are some possible questions:

Is that statement 100% true? (After being told you need a _____or else____(something bad will happen)).

That dowsing question is short and might yield accurate answers, but detailed is better.

If I do not_____(do as suggested) today, will the negative outcome he predicts take place in the time frame he is saying?

Sometimes people stretch things a bit. Maybe you do need a new furnace, but you can get by for a while. And if you have a while, maybe you can put more funds together.

Another issue is wondering if that huge estimate is accurate, or maybe it's been padded. Dowse this:

Is the price quoted for _____(name the job) a competitive and honest price for the quality of work he intends to do?

Remember technique is vital. You must be in a dowsing state to get a good dowsing answer. So do the dowsing lesson in the Resources section before trying to dowse things like this.

32. Replace the ink cartridge?

This is one I've used a lot. It would be nice to always have a couple spare printer cartridges on hand, but sometimes you forget, or you are just pinching pennies, and you have no cartridges ahead. And you just got a warning from the printer that the ink is low.

In your experience, even when you get the warning, you're good for a period of time before the ink runs out. But you use the printer for your business or some project, and so you really want it to be functional when you need it. And maybe the store is a 30-minute drive, and you don't want to make a trip into town just for ink.

You're planning on shopping today, but it is inconvenient for whatever reason to go to the store that sells the cartridges you need. You'd rather wait until next week. But you just aren't sure the ink will last until then. You can't even predict exactly how much you'll need to use the printer. So you have no real idea what is best. This is the ideal time to dowse.

Here's a question you can dowse if you want to wait 7 days to buy the new cartridge:

Considering the usage I will be giving the printer in the next 7 days (you don't have to know what this will be), will the ink in the current cartridge last long enough to do all the printing jobs I will require in the coming 7 days at the quality level I find acceptable?

If you get 'no', buy a new cartridge when you're out shopping today.

∾

33. Total shopping bill

This is an especially useful dowsing application when your budget is tight. In the past, when the balances in our accounts were not that huge, I would want to know how much money to shift into our personal account on shopping day. I wanted only to shift a bit more than enough to buy what I had on my list. But how could I determine that?

If you're good with numbers, you can look at your list and maybe estimate pretty closely. That's what I'd do before I was a dowser. And much of the time, it went ok. But there were too many times when I guessed wrong, and if you don't have enough money in your account and you're out shopping, then you have to find a bank.

Of course these days you can transfer funds using your iPhone, but it's still a nuisance. So why not dowse the answer? We've found this to be a very practical and useful dowsing application, and of course, you get pretty fast confirmation of your accuracy. So make sure your dowsing technique is good.

Make a complete list of the items you want to shop for today.
Then dowse:

Considering the items on my complete shopping list and their availability and price and any other items that I come across that are not on the list that I feel compelled to buy, what will the total be for my purchases today? Over $100? Over $200?

Keep asking until you bracket the numbers, and then you can narrow it down further if you wish. If you dowse 'yes', it will be over $100, but less than $200, then ask Over $110? Over $120? Etc.

It's always terrific to dowse about things you can confirm. So when you get home, add up the expenditures and see how close you were. This number and money dowsing is something that has improved over time for us. So don't be discouraged if at first you are not that great at it. Maybe you have fears about being wrong and what that will mean. Or maybe you have issues with dowsing about money. If either of those is true, do some work to shift that energy.

34. Choose the best car

A car is a major purchase no matter how you look at it. Even if you have a lot of money, you want to make a good choice. You may know in general what you think you like, and that is good. But you probably have a lot of questions you cannot answer. And among them are questions that may not be answered candidly by the seller. Dowsing comes to your rescue!

You are a unique individual, and your priorities will differ from other people's. So make a list of what you want in a car, including:

- Price or monthly payment
- Reliability
- Comfort
- Ease of handling
- Roadworthiness
- How it looks
- Value of the guarantee or warranty
- Resale value
- Suitability for your needs and plans

Of course you may have other things that matter to you, such as color, style, etc. Just make a complete list of the things you care most about.

Then go looking and find a few cars that you think will meet your requirements. It's easier to dowse several candidates that you have come up with using your rational mind than to dowse a huge list of possible cars without using your left brain. We like to encourage people to do their due diligence with their rational mind and then dowse, rather than use dowsing as a replacement for research and due diligence.

Considering all of my goals and priorities for wanting to purchase a car, how does this particular car rate on a scale of 0 to 10, with 10 being really terrific? Is it an 8 or higher?

Remember when dowsing scales, we recommend you pick a cutoff point for action. In buying something, we think 8 or higher is the cutoff. Don't invest in something that's only a 4.

How can you tell what the number is? You can run through the numbers from 0 to 10 slowly out loud or in your head after asking the question, expecting a 'yes' response at the right answer. Or you can do as suggested above and just ask if it's over an 8 on a scale of 10.

We have found that if something ranks as high as an 8, we will usually be happy with it. However, you will be able to tell with practice what number is the best cutoff for you.

~

35. Which item?

This one is really useful. Back before we were dowsers, we occasionally had some real bad luck when buying something at Costco or somewhere that had a stack of boxes, and you just picked one out of the stack and took it home. Have you ever wondered how you managed to pick the only lemon? Or if all of them were lemons?

With dowsing you can avoid the irritation of getting a lemon when you make a purchase. All the boxes look alike. You can't tell just by looking what the best one to choose is. You know not to pick a damaged box, because that item was handled roughly or dropped. But beyond that, you're clueless.

We're assuming you already did your due diligence, and that buying this item is a good move for you. The dowsing is to help you avoid lemons in this case, not make a good decision otherwise.

State in your mind what your intentions are. Example: that you want to choose the item that will perform as good or better than advertised and reliably for the longest possible time. Or define a non-lemon however you wish. Just be specific.

Then use dowsing to find the best item/box within your reach. The boxes are usually stacked in columns or rows, so it's a lot like list dowsing or dowsing items on a shelf. Go to each row or column, asking the question until you get a 'yes', then ask the next question of each box until you find one that gives a 'yes' answer.

Are any of the items in this row/column a 10 on a scale of 0 to 10, with 10 being best, for performing as good or better than advertised, reliably and for the longest possible time?

When you get a 'yes', ask this question of each box in that column or row:

Is this one a 10 using those criteria?

When you get a 'yes', that's the one to buy. And of course, this is a situation that will confirm your dowsing accuracy.

36. Best fishing spot

This is an application that will thrill a sportsman. We don't fish, but if you do, you may prefer to spend your time in a location where you are likely to catch some fish. It isn't always easy to guess where that may be. (OK, we know that for some people, fishing is just an excuse to drink, but for those of you who want to bring home fish, this is a cool dowsing application.)

You can either map dowse or list dowse in a situation like this. Say you have a map that shows the lake or stream you want to fish. You can think about your goals...maybe you want to catch at least 3 fish today and be the only one at that particular spot. Or perhaps you want to catch one fish of a certain size.

Trace the length of the stream slowly with your finger, or travel across or around the lake while asking your dowsing question, and stopping if you get a 'yes'.

Considering my goals for my fishing trip today, please give me a 'yes' when my finger points to a location on this map that will fulfill all of my goals.

This is a bit different from some other dowsing, but it's kind of like free-form list dowsing. You can turn it into a list dowsing exercise in some cases. If you can list the places you are considering fishing by their names or geographic locations, like Morgan's Point or the SW corner of the lake near the reed bed, you can list dowse them instead of using the map. Or you can draw sections/quadrants on the map and dowse each section. It's a matter of personal preference. Lots of times, there won't be names to the locations you are considering, which would make it hard, if not impossible. But if you can make a list, ask this question:

Of all the places on this list, will any fulfill all my goals for today's fishing trip?

If you get 'yes', then go down the list and ask:

Is this one a 'yes'?

Then when you have determined all the good places, you can rank them if you like. Maybe some would allow you to catch 6 fish, while others may be more peaceful and beautiful. You can use a scale of 0 to

10 for the 'yes' places, with 10 being excellent. Just ask for each of the good locations:

On a scale of 0 to 10, with 10 being perfect for my goals, how does
_____*(name the location or point to it on the map) rate? 8 or higher? 5 or higher?*

We tend to use 8 as the cutoff for investing time, effort or money.

37. The best wine

If you drink wine, you know what you like in general. You may even have some favorite brands you frequently buy. But maybe you have a special occasion or just feel like trying something new and different tonight. And you want to select something great from among the many bottles on the shelves at the store.

It's tempting to think that the more you pay, the better the wine will be. To some extent, that is true. But there are remarkable exceptions, and even within a given price range, quality varies radically. And you don't want to buy something that tastes bad.

You really can't be sure how your purchase will turn out if you only use your rational mind. So once you've narrowed it in terms of basics like red or white, or pinot noir or merlot, dowsing can help you pick a great wine for whatever price you are able to pay. We've rarely seen this fail (although dowsing is not 100%, and yes, we have had some disappointments, but not that often).

Before you dowse, focus on what you'd like the wine to be. Make a mental list. Is price important? Lack of negative side effects from drinking a certain amount? Should it go with a particular main course? Do you want to please a particular person with it?

This is a time when you need to do deviceless dowsing. You don't want to pull a pendulum out in public. At least, most people don't. So use the body sway or blink dowsing to get your yes/no response. See the earlier chapter "Tools Or Not?" for a description of The Body Sway, a simple deviceless technique.

Once you have clearly in mind all the things you wish to accomplish, then point your finger at a row of bottles and ask:

Overall for my goals, including price, are there any bottles in this row that are a 8 or better on a scale of 0 to 10, with 10 being best?

You can ask for a 10 if there are a lot of choices. Use your judgment. When you get a 'yes', you can look the bottle over, check the price, and verify by dowsing again what that bottle ranks overall for your goals. If it is 8 or better, it's worth buying.

You may get many responses, so if you do, raise the bar and ask for only 10s. If you still get too many, your list of goals is probably too short. Think more carefully about everything you want that wine to be and ask again. Then buy the best bottle and enjoy!

∽

38. A ripe avocado

Avocados can be a real pain. They can be rather expensive and a big disappointment. Sometimes they have blemishes or are ruined through and through, and you never could tell because of the leathery, hard skin.

Dowsing can help you avoid avocado karma. This same technique works for melons and just about any other type of produce you can think of. Gone will be the times when you paid for produce, then had to throw it out and figure out a replacement for your recipe or meal.

For us, the avocado is the perfect example of how dowsing saves you money and disappointment in the grocery store. So give this a try next time you are picking produce of any kind.

As always, think about why you want the avocado. What do you intend to do with it? What matters most to you? Do you want it blemish-free? Would you like it to be a perfect ripeness by Thursday to use in a meal? Do you want it to be full of vitamins and good taste? Make a mental note of each goal.

You can start with a simple question to determine if any of the avocados in the pile are worth your effort:

Are any of the avocados in this pile an 8 or better on a scale of 0 to 10, with 10 being the best for my goals overall?

If you get 'no', then you need to go to another store. If you get 'yes', then you need to find one or more that will suit your needs. This is another time when deviceless dowsing is appropriate. Check the earlier chapter called "Tools Or Not?" to learn a simple technique. Then ask while pointing to each avocado:

Is this avocado an 8 or better on a scale of 0 to 10, with 10 being best overall for my goals?

You may of course use the number 10 as your goal if there are a lot of avocados. That might help limit the 'yes' answers. When you find any that give a 'yes' response, buy them, and then make sure to see if your dowsing was correct.

Another trick you can use that might seem weird is this. If you aren't sure when you intend to use the avocado, but you would like to get one that will be ripe and perfect for whenever you decide to use it, you can include that in your goals, instead of stating a particular day. So instead of thinking that you want it ripe on Thursday, just focus on picking one that will be ripe whatever day you decide to use it. This also has worked out well for us in the past.

39. Is the steak done?

Unless you are a vegetarian, steak is often considered a very special meal. Good steak is expensive, and you want to cook it to perfection. If you are having a barbecue or dinner party, it becomes even more important to cook the steaks the way your guests like them.

Cooking steak is tricky, because they continue to cook for some time after you remove them from the heat. Sometimes it's hard to calibrate the heat in an outdoor barbecue, which makes it harder to estimate when the steak is done.

Of course you can use a meat thermometer, and if you wish, please do that. But some people don't have one or prefer not to use one. Dowsing is a great substitute. In this case, you just ask:

If I remove this steak from the grill now, will it be cooked exactly the way _____(name of person) likes it when he/she eats it?

Or perhaps you got distracted, and now you are unsure if the steak is actually overcooked. In that case, ask:

Is this steak currently overdone for _____(name person) if I remove it from the grill at this time?

You can also dowse how long to leave something on the heat before removing it:

How long should I continue to cook this steak at this heat level in order to have it cooked exactly to _____(name person)'s taste when he/she eats it? 1 minute? 2 minutes? 3 minutes?

When you get a 'yes', set a timer for that amount and then take the steak off when it dings.

5

Animals & Pets

40. Why isn't she eating?

If your dog (or cat) goes off her food for long, that can be cause for concern. Maybe she's ill. Or perhaps she has gotten something toxic in her system. Or maybe she doesn't like the food or it's gone bad (we've actually experienced this). Since she can't tell you, you don't know what to do.

Dowsing is for getting yes/no answers, so how can it help in this situation? Since dowsing is always about asking yes/no questions, you have to form yes/no questions for this subject, and that can be a bit challenging.

What we would suggest is that you make a list of all the possible things you think might be going on. Here are some examples:

- Indigestion from nonlethal causes, like eating dirt
- Toxic exposure, like to rat poison
- Problems with teeth or gums
- Illness

- Ulcer
- Trauma
- Hairball
- Food allergy or sensitivity
- Food spoiled
- Food not to her liking
- Other

Always add 'other' to any list you make, because no one can think of all the reasons for any symptom. If you get 'other' as the answer, of course that means more head-scratching, but that's ok. Don't be afraid of that. You want to get the truth.

This is a list dowsing situation obviously, so you can use your pendulum or a deviceless technique to go down the list asking, as you point your finger at each item one at a time, slowly:

Is this a significant factor in Fifi's not eating her food at this time?

We define the term 'significant' to be something that is contributing in a big way to the symptom. You don't want a 'yes' for something that is not a big factor. So maybe Fifi doesn't like chicken, but that isn't the main reason she isn't eating. You don't want a 'yes' for something that isn't significant. Be clear in your mind what you mean by 'significant' before you dowse.

Be prepared to check the entire list. There may be more than one reason. Then use either your judgment or dowsing to decide what to do about it. **Always get a second opinion on health issues.**

∽

41. Checking pain level

If you're like us, you love your pets like they're family. You can't stand for them to be in pain. But they can't tell you. Sometimes it's obvious from a limp or a moan. But pain of various kinds can be silent and slowly erode the health and well-being of your best friend, even masking a serious condition until it's too late to treat.

Dowsing is a great way to determine if your animal companion is in pain, and what level of pain she is feeling. Maybe your cat Princess has gotten older, and you are concerned she is arthritic. Or else she is acting a bit 'off' and you want to make sure she isn't suffering.

The 0 to 10 scale can be used for determining the level of pain your cat is feeling at a given time. The way we define the scale, a 3 or higher is something that will bother the cat. 8 or higher is something that needs to be investigated and perhaps get a vet's help, because it is seriously intense.

You can ask about what level of pain she feels now, or you can ask for an average over the past several days. You can ask the level one month ago and compare it to the level today. Some conditions cause irregular pain that comes and goes or is related to a specific activity or time of day. The averaging process is best in such cases. We suggest you do both, so that you be sure to get the most information. (You can reword the questions to find what the highest level of pain is that she has experienced in a given time frame).

On a scale of 0 to 10, with 0 being none and 10 being the highest, what level of pain is Princess experiencing in her joints at this time?

On a scale of 0 to 10, with 0 being none, what is the average level of pain that Princess has experienced in her joints in the past 7 days?

On a scale of 0 to 10, with 0 being none, what is the average level of pain that Princess was experiencing in her joints during the seven days of the first week of _____(month and year, in the past)?

You can use your results to determine if the pain is getting worse over time. It will tell you if it is constant or comes and goes. It will also give you the level of intensity so you can decide if you need to get outside help or investigate further. You can drop the specific 'in her joints' phrase and just dowse pain level in her body overall if you aren't sure where the pain is.

Always get a second opinion on health issues.

42. The best toy

Those of us who regard our pets as family love to buy them toys. But toys seem to be getting more and more expensive, and maybe you've had the experience we have, where you bought a toy for something like $14, and when you gave it to your dog, she didn't show much interest in it, but it was slimed, so you couldn't return it. Money wasted!

Wouldn't it be great to always know that the toy you pick will be loved and used by your dog? Well, with dowsing, that becomes a reality! It's true that dowsing is not 100% accurate, but it increases your chances of success so much, that you won't mind the rare occasional misfire. You will save so much money and disappointment with dowsing that you will simply be grateful. As grateful as your pet will be!

Think about what you want your dog to do with a toy. Do you want her to play with it consistently for a certain time period? Do you want her to really like it? Do you have concerns that it be safe for her? Do you want it to give her chewing opportunities or allow you to enjoy playing together? Make a mental list of all the things you want the toy to be. Then ask:

Are any of these toys an 8 or better overall for my goals on a scale of 0 to 10, with 10 being best?

Maybe your dog won't like any of those toys. If you can't get a 'yes', don't waste your money. We always want an 8 or higher before investing in anything. Go to another store, website or catalog and try again. Or maybe your dog just isn't in the mood for a toy and would rather have a dog treat or biscuit.

If you get that 'yes', there are toys that are 8 or higher, use The Body Sway (from the chapter "Tools Or Not?") or a pendulum if you don't mind stares, and point to the toys, asking this question of each one until you get one or more 'yes' answers:

Is this toy an 8 or higher on a scale of 0 to 10, with 10 being perfect for my goals at this time as a toy for ____(pet's name)?

You can either stop at the first 'yes' or get a few and then dowse for a 10 if you like. If you get too many 'yes' answers, you probably haven't listed clear enough goals. Go back and do that again.

43. Pet compatibility

If you are an animal lover like we are, you may find yourself wanting more than one pet. But you've heard stories of how badly that can turn out. Sometimes bringing a young pup in will rejuvenate an older dog; other times it will aggravate him. Often, an older cat will have no patience for a puppy, but sometimes it will welcome the company.

Animals, like people, are unique. You cannot easily predict for sure when they will or won't get along.

There are many possible negative scenarios. It is true that very elderly animals often don't like rambunctious young ones brought into the family. They may be frail and hurting and unwilling to be patient with the craziness. Cats that have had bad experiences with dogs will not welcome a dog to the family.

It's usually easier to adopt 2 cats from a litter and get compatibility than to bring a second cat in after having one for a long time. A kitten and a puppy raised together will usually get along easier than when one is brought in after the other is an adult.

Many animals are territorial about their home and their people. Don't assume they want company. But it's generally true that if you spend much time away from home, your single pet will be less happy. Animals tend to be social. It's usually easier if you bring two animals in together than if you add one later on.

Dowsing will help you determine if the puppy you want to adopt will be accepted and get along ok with your cat. Here are some questions you can ask, depending on your goals (change the wording to suit your situation):

If I adopt this puppy at this time, will my cat be happy to have the puppy join the family?

If I adopt this puppy at this time, will my cat accept the puppy within 2 months time?

If I adopt this puppy at this time, will my cat grow to love it within 3 months?

If I adopt this puppy at this time, will my cat begin to show bad behavior like fighting and spraying? If yes, will the bad behavior be easy to correct?

If I adopt this puppy at this time, will my cat's life be enhanced?

Of course you may use a 0 to 10 scale to determine the intensity of the good or bad reaction your cat will have. Just include the usual phrase in your question.

∾

44. Dental issues

One of my first major dowsing projects was to evaluate the physical health of my pets. I made a list of organs, systems and conditions, and I dowsed for my horse and my dog. I kept a record of the results. Both of them dowsed as being in good condition except for their dental health.

This was perplexing, because I was unaware that anything was wrong. I had even had my horse's teeth examined and floated by a vet shortly after buying him. It seemed that perhaps my dowsing was wrong. But it's important to trust your dowsing, so I started doing some research. Not surprisingly, within a couple weeks, I was informed about a presentation by an equine dentist, a specialist in dental care for horses. After going to his presentation, I realized that my dowsing was probably correct, so I made an appointment.

Even though my horse had had his teeth floated by a vet, the equine dentist found some major problems because he used techniques that were better at allowing him to get into the horse's mouth. Upon treatment, my horse suddenly was willing for the first time to let me slip the bridle and bit on him easily. Apparently, he had been in pain and was trying to tell me by pulling away when I tried to tack him up. The cowboy who owned the boarding facility had said my horse was just taking advantage of me, a green owner. Boy, was he wrong!

These results encouraged me to make an appointment with a veterinary dentist. Another interesting coincidence had placed him on my radar due to an article in the Phoenix paper about his work with the big cats at the zoo.

My dog, who was several years old, had broken a canine tooth trying to get out of her crate when she was less than a year old. The vet I had at the time had said no problem, but the specialist discovered an abscess on it. The veterinary dentist said it was the biggest abscess he'd ever seen, and that she had been in pain her whole life since the abscess first developed. I felt really bad!

I remembered how as a puppy, Tammi had loved kids, but when she matured and was about a year or so old, she started pulling away from their hugs. I had attributed it to the Akita personality. After the dental work, Tammi let my niece cuddle and hug her for the first time. It was obvious her shrinking from kids and even warning them was quite restrained, considering the pain their touch must have caused…

Your animals cannot tell you except by their behavior what's bothering them. It's always best to assume that their misbehavior is not wanton, but a way of saying they are scared or in pain or need your help. Yet too often, we fail to see misbehavior as a plea for help. What a shame!

Dowsing helps you restore a better attitude towards your pet's behavior, as it empowers you to see what the cause is for that 'acting out'.

You must use yes/no questions, and there are many ways of doing it, but here are several that will give you a start:

Is _____'s (name the pet) misbehavior (name the specific behavior) due in any part to physical pain?

Is _____'s (name the pet) misbehavior (name the specific behavior) due in any part to fear or phobia?

On a scale of 0 to 10, with 0 being none and 10 being the most he/she can experience, what is the level of fear/pain my pet is experiencing when displaying this symptom?

On a 0 to 10 scale, with 0 being horrible and 10 being excellent, how does the dental health of my pet rate at this time?

If the number is below 8, his/her dental health is not that great. If it is below 5, you might want to have a professional examine him/her. If you got that there was pain and that dental health is low, definitely seek a second opinion.

45. Separation anxiety

Separation anxiety was unnamed when we were young pet owners, but we saw its ugly consequences in our lonely pets. I had several dogs when I was in my 20s who were left alone at home most of the day, and they would chew things due to anxiety. I remember one day coming home to find my dog had pulled the baseboards off the wall and chewed them, which was kind of the last straw. Records, books and furniture had been destroyed before that. This behavior made the dogs appear to be bad dogs, but they couldn't help it. Yet the destruction was terrible and expensive, and caused damage to our relationship, because of the pressure it put on me.

Years later, separation anxiety was defined, and there are now ways to treat it. Most of all, people are becoming aware that dogs are social beings who should not be left in the yard or house alone all day. They need a job and companionship, or they go a bit crazy. They need lots of exercise, too.

What can you do if in spite of your best intentions, you have to leave your dog at home alone for long periods of time? You can follow all the suggestions from the experts about separation anxiety, but you may wonder how much your dog is suffering. He may not be eating your couch, but you are concerned if your efforts have mitigated the worst effects of loneliness.

Dowsing is very useful to finding out things your dog can't tell you.

On a scale of 0 to 10, with 0 being none and 10 being the most he could feel, how much separation anxiety on the average does _____(name of dog) experience while I am away for more than 2/3/4 hours (fill in with an appropriate amount of time) at this time (meaning currently as opposed to in the past)?

Beware of not being in a dowsing state with this question. You want to have a good answer. You may not want to know the truth, as you feel you've done all you can, and what will you do if the answer is bad? But you must adopt a curious attitude and be open to hearing ANYTHING, because what use is dowsing if you only want it to tell you what you want?

∾

46. Your pet's physical condition

As your dog ages, you may be concerned about how much walking is healthy for him. Maybe it helps his heart rate and exercises his muscles, but what about the strain on his joints, especially in hilly areas? What about hot, humid weather? Does that put too much strain on his system?

You may have some vague intuition about what to do, but dowsing is a sort of focused intuition that allows you to get clear and useful answers to these questions. Here are some that you might ask:

Considering my dog's age and physical condition, the weather and the proposed path we would take, will taking _____(dog's name) on this walk at this time have an overall positive effect on his health and well-being?

That's a way to ask it without using a scale, like 0 to 10, but of course, you can use a scale if you want more detail:

On a scale of 0 to 10, with 0 being harmful and 10 being very healthy, what does taking _____(dog's name) on this walk at this time rate overall for his health and well-being?

∼

47. Animal communication

If you love animals like we do, you want to be able to talk to them. You wish they could talk back. But you don't picture yourself as an animal communicator. You've seen them. They are exotic and talented and psychic. And you aren't. But with dowsing, you can become an animal communicator quite easily.

With your pet's permission, you can conduct a conversation with her using dowsing. Of course, it's a bit slower than some forms of animal communication, but it's easier to learn and use. And anyone can do it.

Permission is the first thing. Not all animals want to converse with you. So ask them first.

Would you (or name the animal, if not present; you can do this long distance) be willing to answer some questions for me?

If you get 'no', do not proceed. If you get 'yes', you may start.

At first, you may find it easier to ask simple questions:

Do you love me?

Do you like the kibble I feed you?

Do you like your_____(name a toy)?

Do you like_____(name another pet or child in the family)?

Do you like the taste of the water I give you? (Animals generally do not like unfiltered tap water)

Do you like the dog park/where we go for walks/throwing your ball outside?

Be prepared, because you might get some surprises. In fact, if you don't get surprising answers, and you've asked a lot of questions, you may not really be dowsing. Surprising or unexpected answers should turn up now and then. They are a way of seeing that you are actually open to the truth, and you are not providing the answers yourself. If you never get a surprising answer when dowsing, you probably aren't really dowsing.

You may go on to ask harder questions about how your dog feels physically; how it feels when you go away; if she would like to participate in an obedience or agility class; if she likes the vet. Use your imagination and be sure to define your terms carefully. Such questions are harder to form into yes/no questions, but it can be done if you break it down into several questions instead of one.

～

48. Improving your breeding program

Animal breeding is a complex subject and doing it well requires a lot of knowledge and experience about biology, energy and the breed of animal you are working with, as well as clear and ethical goals for the offspring of any breeding. It is too complex a subject to deal with in a single question or page. We suggest you get the Whole Brain Charts mentioned in the Resources section, as one of them is a complete breeding chart that you can use to improve the results in your breeding program.

For the purposes of this book, there are some dowsing questions that can get you started for improving your breeding program. The physical, mental and emotional condition of the breeding pair is of paramount concern. We have seen mothers reject babies and breedings lead to miscarriages when these things were ignored. Dowsing helps you see if your animals are in condition to breed. For the females, ask:

Does _____(name the animal) want to have a baby in the coming year (or name the time frame)?

Is _____(name the animal) in excellent physical condition for being bred at this time?

Is _____(name the animal) physically capable of carrying a pregnancy to term and having a healthy baby at this time (or over the appropriate time frame)?

Is _____(name the animal) mentally and emotionally capable of carrying a pregnancy to term and being a good mother?

Is _____(name the animal) a good match genetically with _____(name the sperm donor) for producing healthy offspring that meet all my program goals? (Be sure you have a list of goals)

For the males, ask:

Is _____(name the animal) a good overall match with_____(name the female) for producing offspring that will meet all the goals of my breeding program?

Is_____(name the animal) capable of breeding with _____(name the female) at this time and producing healthy offspring?

Will artificial insemination of_____(name the female) on _____(date) with the sperm of _____ *(name the animal), frozen on* _____ *(date) produce healthy offspring that meet all the goals of my breeding program?*

If you can't find anything that meets all the goals, you can lower your standards and say 80% or more of my goals, etc.

This is obviously just a small sample of the things you can do with dowsing to improve your breeding program.

$\sim$

49. Find a good trainer

Horse trainers come in all types. Sadly, some are very hard on horses. We had a client whose mare was traumatized so much by a trainer that she would attack any man who came close to her if she had the opportunity. (Nigel turned his back on the mare and she bit the heck out of him.) But it isn't just abuse you want to avoid. You want to pick a trainer whose style, values and personality match your horse and will make training pleasant and enjoyable as well as successful. Plus price matters.

Dowsing is one of the only ways you can have confidence in picking a trainer. Make a list of all your goals, including those above. Then be sure to adopt a curious attitude when you dowse. Put aside any bias or preconceived notions you have. Be open to hearing the best choice for your goals. Then dowse each trainer candidate:

On a scale of 0 to 10, with 0 being terrible and 10 being excellent, how does _____ *(name of trainer) rate overall for my goals as a trainer for* _____ *(name the horse) at this time (or name other time frame)?*

Remember that we suggest you only take action when the number is 8 or higher. Be prepared to find out that no one is an 8. If not, get some more candidates. Trust your dowsing. It can save you time and money, your horse's well-being and health.

This same basic approach can be applied to any type of animal trainer or training program.

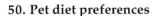

50. Pet diet preferences

When you buy pet food of any kind, you are buying what looks good to you. You base your choice on your values and goals. But you don't know how your animal companion will like it. Most dogs will eat whatever you put in front of them, but cats are pretty finicky about taste. And if you are buying good quality food, you don't want it to be unappreciated.

Dowsing is a way of finding out how your pet regards the food and water you give him. Not how healthy it is for him. Dowsing can find that out, too, but in this example, we're talking about preferences. Plain and simple. Does he like it? And how much? Because you want him to like it a lot.

This question, like many in this book, uses a scale to give shades of yes and no. For this one, let's try a +10 to -10 scale, because this question asks for a positive or negative or neutral judgment. It will be an easier scale to interpret.

On a scale of +10 to -10, with negative numbers meaning dislike and bigger numbers meaning more intense, how much does _____(name the pet) like the food I am feeding him at this time? Positive? 0? Negative? (Then drill down to find the individual rating).

On a scale of +10 to -10, with negative numbers meaning dislike and bigger numbers meaning more intense, how much does _____(name the pet) like the water I am giving him at this time? Positive? 0? Negative? (Then drill down to get the exact value by saying each number).

Animals have strong noses and keen tastes, and they have the ability to detect chemicals in tap water, and this causes them to drink less, which is actually unhealthy. Many types of pet food have additives, preservatives and ingredients that are not palatable, or they may have ingredients that are not healthy that have been added to make them palatable. These questions will only show your animal's like or dislike. 0 is neutral. Positive number is liking, and negative numbers is dislike.

You also need to take into account that sometimes there are palatability factors added to overcome bad ingredients. Beet pulp is a useless ingredient used to sweeten horse feed and cover up less-than-healthy ingredients. Your animal can become addicted to some of these things, just like you can get addicted to sugar. So you might want to differentiate between liking something that's healthy and liking something that's meant to be addictive or flavor-enhancing, but might not be healthy.

Do your best to be detached and don't expect or want certain answers. Dowsing gives surprising answers sometimes. But when you trust them, you can be amazed at the results.

∾

51. Favorite treats

It's always fun to give treats to your animal companion. And almost anything will do. Carrots and apples for horses, bones for dogs. But if you love your animals as much as we love ours, you really want to give them treats they go crazy for. And although you can tell when they don't like something, it's harder to tell what their favorite is. And if you see a new style of treat, you hesitate, because you aren't sure they'll like it.

Dowsing comes to the rescue again! You can dowse how much your furry best friend will like the treat you are contemplating buying. You can use a scale of 0 to 10, with 8 as the cutoff point for buying, or you can ask a simple question that compares the new treat to an old favorite. Here are some possible dowsing questions:

Will _____(name of animal) like _____(name of treat)

as well or better than she currently likes_____(name of favorite known treat)?

On a scale of 0 to 10, with 0 being not at all, how much will _____(name of animal) like_____(name of treat)? 10? 9? 8? Lower? (Don't buy it unless it's at least an 8).

Remember to be curious and detached when asking the question. You may have been captivated by the name or concept or look of the new treat. Put aside your preferences and be open to hearing the actual truth.

When dowsing scales, remember that you can dowse each number on the scale if you wish. After saying the question, then ask, "Is it a 0?", "Is it a 1?", etc, until you get a yes. Or you can just ask if the item is an 8 or higher and be done with it in one question.

Our book on intuitive animal care is great if you want to dive further into the subject of having a better relationship with your animal companion. You can find it at the Sixth Sense Books site, with links to all major online retailers.

6

Gardening

52. Evaluating plant needs

Dowsing is a useful adjunct to a green thumb, and it is downright necessary if you don't have one. There are so many things in gardening that are done by 'feel'. You get to know your plants and respond to them instinctively. Still, there are times you won't be sure what to do. Here are some simple basic questions that you can use when you aren't sure the best course of action for a plant that appears to be in ill health.

We're going to use a scale of +10 to -10 here, because it is quite useful in terms of measuring too much or too little or just right. You use this scale just as you do the 0 to 10 scale, asking the question and then naming each number (or a group of numbers, like 'positive numbers'), while waiting for a 'yes' response.

The questions here will be used to determine if the plant needs more or less water, sunlight or fertilizer. Often, when a plant looks bad, the symptoms for overwatering and underwatering are identical. These questions pinpoint what actions to take to restore health.

Considering the needs of this plant at this time, on a scale of +10 to -10, with 0 being perfect, positive numbers meaning too much and negative numbers meaning too little, how is the amount of water it is getting?

Considering the needs of this plant at this time, on a scale of +10 to -10, with 0 being perfect, positive numbers meaning too much and negative numbers meaning too little, how is the amount of sunlight it is getting?

Considering the needs of this plant at this time, on a scale of +10 to -10, with 0 being perfect, positive numbers meaning too much and negative numbers meaning too little, how is the amount of fertilizer it is getting?

You can think of ways to create new questions to check out other variables that may be of concern. Record your answers and follow through. Then watch for results to confirm your dowsing.

∾

53. What to plant?

If you are planting a garden of any kind, you will need to select what varieties of flowers or plants to use. Your experience and preferences will go a long way to helping you choose the best ones, but sometimes you are faced with a decision that you can't make rationally. Maybe you want to try a new variety of squash, and what you've read hasn't really helped you decide if it would work out well in your garden.

You can use dowsing to help you choose. Make a list of the things that matter. What do you want to consider that could affect success with this variety of squash? Tolerance of sunlight? Susceptibility to disease? Problems with humidity? Make a list of the factors that you need this squash to do well on in order for it to be a good choice for your garden. Then dowse:

Considering my goals for this vegetable in my garden, is the _____(name variant) an 8 or better on a scale of 10, with 10 being most successful for planting this season?

Notice how this time instead of asking each number, we just go for 8 or better, because we know we aren't investing in anything that rates lower. You can make all your scale questions of this type like that.

Dowsing has helped us avoid disappointment so many times, we've lost count. And many decisions involve time, effort and money, so dowsing is a truly valuable resource.

∼

54. Where to plant?

Unless you are a truly experienced gardener or have had a lot of education in horticulture, you don't always know the exact best place to plant something in your garden. Plus, even if you know the theory, that isn't always enough. Sometimes there are just 'bad' spots to plant, where no plant could thrive, for any number of reasons, but it isn't obvious when looking at them.

Dowsing therefore becomes a useful tool for any level of gardener who wants to avoid failure. It's terrible to plant a tree or shrub and then watch it die in spite of your best efforts, because the spot you chose just isn't right for it.

This type of dowsing can be done with a sketch of your garden while you sit at the kitchen table, or you can walk around the garden, pointing to possible planting spots. It's your choice. If you choose the latter, a single L-rod is a useful dowsing tool. It can point to a location as well as give you a yes/no answer. If you choose to dowse over a sketch, you will benefit from reading up on map dowsing. See the Resources section for the link to Discovering Dowsing, where you can find Map Dowsing under Techniques. Map dowsing is not hard to learn, but as we've mentioned, this isn't a book on technique, so we'll just list the question you can dowse outdoors in the garden with your L-rod.

You can go outside and stand in your garden and define the

boundaries. Define within the boundaries where the places you are able to plant are located. This is important, because you may have some spots within the garden that you cannot dig due to buried services, or that aren't convenient, like under a bench or in the middle of some hardscaping. Make it clear what areas you are open to planting in. Then ask the following question:

Considering all the needs and preferences of this particular plant, including sunlight, water, drainage and any other important factor for its health, please point at the location in this garden that is available for planting that this plant would most likely thrive in.

Let the L-rod swing and point to a particular location. It may even point behind you. (See the videos on Discovering Dowsing for how to hold and use an L-rod). Be sure you are in a dowsing state, and relax and don't try to guess the answer. If you have to move to allow the rod to swing, do so. When it appears to be pointing at one location, double check that this is the best direction to go in. When you get 'yes' ask the following as you walk in that direction:

Please give me a 'yes' when my left foot reaches the best place to plant this particular plant.

The most common 'yes' is the rod swinging towards your chest. If for some reason you never get a 'yes', it could be that the straight line you walked did not cross the correct spot. You may need to walk parallel to that line a few inches out on either side until you find exactly the right spot. Then, confirm your answer by asking:

Is this the best spot to plant this plant?

It can be challenging to trust your dowsing. Obviously, if the location makes absolutely no sense at all and feels all wrong, don't do it. Otherwise, trust your answer and plant the plant. Then watch for confirmation of your answer.

Not that this is dowsing, but when gardening, it can be very useful to work with the nature spirits of the location. They will help you get better results. You can use dowsing to communicate with them using the techniques listed in the pet section for animal communication. Working with nature spirits gives far better gardening results.

55. Dealing with pests

You may have studied about plant pests or have lots of experience, but at some point, we all run into a situation we don't have an answer for. If you have researched and still cannot find the best way to solve your plant pest issue, dowsing might be helpful.

For example, you may have several treatments at hand, or maybe you are contemplating buying something from a catalog or garden store. You can use a dowsing question to find the best solution. Make a list of the possible remedies, and be sure to add 'Other' to the list. This will be a list dowsing exercise, so you might want to re-read that section from the earlier part of the book.

Use this question to dowse the list of solutions and find the best. We suggest using a 0 to 10 scale, with 0 being ineffective and 10 being very effective. Point at each product and ask:

Is this an 8 or better on a scale of 10 for resolving the _____(name the pest) issue in my garden quickly and effectively with no bad side effects?

Make a note of which give an 8. If none do, then you can either look for other possible solutions to dowse, or you can lower your standards. Instead of 'quickly and effectively', you might just say 'effectively'. If you get 'Other' as the best choice, then you have to do more research, but don't let that discourage you, because the work you do up front to pick the best solution will pay off best in the long run.

7

Relationships

56. How compatible are you?

It isn't very romantic, but knowing if you are compatible is a very
important subject if you expect to have a successful relationship of any
kind. But what exactly does compatible mean to you? You need to
think that out very clearly before you do any dowsing.

Some people might be content to know that the person they are
interested in is compatible in a sexual way. Frankly, you don't need
dowsing to tell you that. Most people have good enough intuition that
they know pretty fast. But if you have any maturity at all, you know
that relationships based only on sex are not destined to be long and
satisfying in other ways. So it's wise to include other factors in your
concept of compatibility.

Some of the things you might consider include: similar values &
beliefs, shared interests, personalities that are comfortable together.
Values and beliefs can be a real stumbling block. Whether religious,
political or just basic things like honesty and fidelity or the way you

think about money, a relationship can shatter when it hits the rocks of incompatible values and beliefs. Most people are not interested in compromising such things, and fighting over money, religion, politics, honesty and fidelity gets tiring pretty fast.

Shared interests and personality traits are important, but perhaps not as volcanic when incompatible. Yet two people can drift apart if they don't have things they love to do together. And misunderstandings can be common if their personalities clash. An introvert may seem subversive and anti-social to an extrovert. A thinker may seem cold and uncaring to a feeler.

If you have any interest in a successful long-term friendship, love affair, business venture or marriage, you need to be compatible in all the ways that matter to you. Dowsing will help you predict how compatible you are in a way that just listing what you know cannot. It can be very challenging to trust your dowsing or be detached about this, but it is a great learning experience.

Make a list of the things that matter most to you, the things you would break up with someone over, if they disagreed or acted opposite to what you value. Honesty? Kindness? Gentleness? Loves children or animals? Generous with money? Take your time and think about all the hazards you can think of in relationships, and what you most want in a partner/lover/spouse. Then dowse about him/her. We'll use a scale of +10 to -10, so you can see positive, neutral and negative.

Please note that you can dowse each trait individually for compatibility, such as compatibility on the subject of how to deal with money, or honesty. Start with the overall compatibility measurement, then go to individual subjects if you are interested. This can be especially enlightening if you got a lower number than expected. It may turn out your beloved tests very high for sexual compatibility or romance, but very low on something else that matters to you, and that drags down the overall score.

By looking at individual subjects, you can decide if you want to accept less than an 8 overall (we don't recommend it), but at least you can do it with your eyes open, knowing exactly where the bumps in the road may lie.

Considering all the factors that matter to me in creating a successful relationship, how compatible is _____(name the person) overall on a +10 to -10 scale, with positive numbers being compatible, negative numbers being incompatible and 0 being neutral?

Remember that when using a scale, you can have a written scale you swing a pendulum over while asking this question. The +10 to -10 scale usually resembles a protractor, with 0 at the top of the half-circle, and +10 on the horizontal right side and -10 on the horizontal left side. Start by swinging your pendulum in a neutral swing, in line with the zero (vertically), then allow it to move slowly left or right to settle over the correct number. If it doesn't move at all, the answer is 0.

Acting on what you dowse, if the answer is disappointing, can be very tough. But be open to seeing the truth and acting in your best interests. If in doubt, always get someone to dowse for you or ask a dowsing buddy to dowse the same question and compare answers. This is a very important topic, and a second opinion is a good idea.

57. Marry or not?

Since marriage is one of the most important decisions in anyone's life, and since it is rarely a simple rational choice, dowsing can be useful in confirming your choice (or not). The compatibility score that you got in the last section can be a good foundation for building a successful relationship. When you get to the point of marriage, though, you may find it hard to decide if the contentment or comfort you feel with this person is enough to warrant a lifetime commitment. After all, so many marriages end in divorce, and divorce is so costly in many ways.

Anyone who has any real doubts should not marry. Intuition is powerful enough at important times like this to really give you useful advice. Going with your gut feeling is best. But sometimes you have fears or concerns that drown out the voice of your intuition. Or maybe when you tune in, you don't get any real impressions. Or perhaps the physical passion you feel is so overpowering that you have trouble connecting with the mental or emotional parts of yourself objectively.

It's necessary to be detached if you want to dowse important subjects, which is why the examples in this book go from simple to more challenging. If you jump ahead in the book, you will find yourself overwhelmed and not ready to dowse such important or even life or death subjects. Take your time and work up to it by building confidence in the easier applications early in the book.

What makes a good marriage in your mind? Everyone is unique. Don't use other people's definitions of good marriage. My Mom once said that you shouldn't complain if your husband didn't drink, gamble or beat you or run around on you, especially if he made a decent living. She grew up in an age when men put a roof over your head, and if they followed certain rules, you were expected to act happy, whether you were fulfilled or not. She was not. My Mom was miserable in her marriage, but it gave her the security she did not have as a child during the Depression. Being loved was not a part of it.

Don't accept anyone's definition of a happy marriage but your own. Make your own list and be true to it. Otherwise, you may find yourself locked in a very unhappy situation and feeling trapped. Once you have your list of priorities in a happy marriage written down, dowse using any of these questions:

If I marry _____(name person), how happy will I be overall with my marriage after 5 years, on a scale of +10 to -10, with negative numbers being unhappy, positive numbers being happy and 0 being neutral?

If I marry_____(name person), will it turn out that he is the life partner I have always wanted?

*If I marry _____(name person), will I be happy overall that I did so
for as long as we both live?*

We always say get a second opinion on any major choice, and that's
true for this as well.

58. Divorce or not?

Divorce, like marriage, is a serious subject. Many marriages end in
divorce. It is costly and painful to both partners, any children, the in-
laws, pets and friends of both. The more acrimonious it is, the harder it
is on everyone. Yet sometimes divorce is the absolute right choice to
put people's lives back on a path that can lead to happiness. The cost
can be great, but the rewards can be worth it.

Each person must decide for him/herself what matters most. My Mom
stayed married in spite of being unhappy with my Dad. He had few
vices, but was totally incompatible and emotionally unavailable and
was unempathetic to the challenges she faced. She didn't feel
competent to hold a job, and she was probably right, having tried so
many different types without any long term success. Finally she gave
up and stayed home, but she hated that, too. With her values and her
issues, divorce seemed a bad choice, though tempting, and I can see
why she stuck it out. But I sure couldn't have.

Looking at someone else's choice, you might think it was a dumb
choice to stay or go. But that is based on your values, not theirs. If you
are ever faced with the decision about dissolving your marriage, you
will find how challenging it can be. Friends and family may not
support you; money may seem too scarce; you may fear losing touch
with your kids; you may even be afraid of losing your pet.

Divorce is a very stressful decision and not to be entertained lightly.
You want to do what's best for you. Usually, what's best for you will

end up being best for everyone else, if you are able to be totally honest. That's a big 'if'. It is really hard to be totally honest. Some people would say my Mom should have quit complaining about my Dad and saying she would have left except for us. She should have just left. It did scar me for her to say that to we kids were the reason she stayed in a bad marriage. I could see she was very unhappy. For a time, I was even angry that she stayed and blamed us kids. She was Catholic, and divorce seemed wrong to her. But looking back as an adult, I don't think that was her reason for staying. I think she just intuitively knew she couldn't easily hold a job and support us kids, and that Dad wasn't interested in us and might have avoided supporting us if he could. She wasn't willing to test that, and she had no faith in the courts or her own abilities, so she stayed. I think in retrospect it was a good choice for her, and with all its negative consequences, it would have worked out worse if she had left. But that wouldn't have worked for me.

It's important not to judge based on outward things like what your parents, friends or religion tells you. You need to get in touch with what really matters to you. Listen to your heart. Have the courage to do what is best for you. Dowsing can sometimes give you an extra measure of courage to do something you're afraid of (like when I went to meet Nigel against the advice of almost everyone) or not to do something rash that will turn out worse in the end.

So make a list of the things that matter to you in life. Some are: being loved and cherished, security, respect, support, good communication, personal fulfillment, finances, your children's long term happiness and emotional health, your health, honesty and sharing. Be specific and as complete as possible. Be sure to include anything that is a 'make or break' subject. In other words, if financial security is your #1 priority, include it in the list as such.

Dowse the following questions:

If I divorce_____(name spouse), will I be happy I did so when I reach the end of my life?

Will divorcing_____(name spouse) give me more_____(fill blank with a priority, like financial security or happiness) overall in the long term than I have being married to him/her?

Remember to strive for detachment while dowsing. You must be curious and open to the truth if you want accuracy.

8

Health

Warning: Please read!

If you have skipped ahead to this section of the book without taking our dowsing course (see the Resources) and without serious practice at simpler dowsing applications, we urge you NOT to proceed. The applications in this book go from simple to complicated. We designed it to be a journey of discovery and building confidence without negative side effects. Health dowsing is a serious topic and not to be undertaken by novices.

Remember that dowsing is not 100% accurate. No method is. But anything to do with health requires a second opinion, sometimes a third.

Be warned that dowsing for health is a way of empowering you to become more involved in your health, but it is NOT meant to take the place of your health care provider.

∾

59. Choose a nutritional supplement

Dowsing nutritional supplements is probably THE most commonly used application of dowsing that we have seen over the years. However, since most people have not had a good dowsing course, they are not aware how to properly form a question that will give a useful answer. So that's what we will share here.

Vitamins are expensive, at least any that are worth anything. So you don't want to waste money, do you? Dowsing will absolutely save you a TON of money when picking supplements. Your left brain will be looking at labels and advertising claims and maybe even the articles you've read online, or possibly even the suggestion of a health care professional. You might be wondering as your chiropractor suggests a particularly expensive product he sells, if that really would work for you.

Deep down in your heart, you know that nothing works for everyone. Dowsing is the best way to find out what works for you.

In the case of being told to buy a particular supplement for a certain goal, like to clear up the cause of a symptom, you can dowse this question:

On a scale of 0 to 10, with 0 being no effect, and 10 being the most positive, how does _____(name the specific brand and supplement) rate for resolving the cause(s) of _____(name symptom or condition)?

Or you could just ask:

On a scale of 0 to 10, with 0 being no effect, and 10 being the most positive, does _____(name the specific brand and supplement) rate 8 or higher for resolving the cause(s) of _____(name symptom or condition)?

The first question requires you do dowse each number from 0 to 10 until you get a 'yes', or to dowse groups of numbers, like 0-5. The second question acknowledges you won't buy anything that tests less than 8, and goes straight for a 'yes' or 'no'.

Do NOT allow yourself to become attached to a certain answer. Don't let your rational mind try to guess, or your fear of spending block you. Remember to be totally curious and just wait for the correct answer. You don't have to act on it, so don't borrow trouble.

You can modify the above questions when dowsing a catalog or in a store to find the best supplement for your goal. Remember, as always, you need a clear goal. And if the goal is to restore health, treating causes is more effective than suppressing symptoms. You can ask for the best pain relief, but that won't cure the cause. And the supplement or remedy for each might be quite different.

Never use simple questions like, "Is this supplement good for me?" The word 'good' is too vague, and no goal has been specified. Even if you set up a goal ahead of asking, and define 'good', you still won't get as clear an answer as if you use a more detailed question.

$\sim$

60. Test for food allergies

There are many types of tests for allergies, but none of them is perfect. While we always say check with your health care professional about any health concern, if you are a competent and confident dowser, you can check yourself for allergies and sensitivities by dowsing.

Allergies and sensitivities are similar in how they present in terms of symptoms, but they are different in terms of health definition. So we include both terms in our questions, so as not to miss anything. We will refer to allergies from now on with the understanding that we include sensitivities in that term.

You may find yourself allergic to things you breathe, things you eat or drink (ingest) and things you contact. In some cases, an allergen may affect you through more than one of these routes. For example, particles of fiberglass insulation that have been put into the air due to cutting pieces in an enclosed space with a band saw may be breathed AND may also land on your skin and create a reaction. Contact and inhalation are the routes in that case.

We use a 0 to 10 scale to measure the level of intensity of allergy/sensitivity to a substance. Zero means no reaction, while 10 is the worst. Anything over a 3 is a reaction that will be noticeable. Anything 8 or higher needs to be eliminated from your environment or diet.

An interesting concept we won't go into depth about here is that you can have an allergic reaction to an emotion, a concept, a situation. For example: you can be allergic to power, good health, being loved, wealth. These can be tested in the same ways as food.

You may have some guesses about what you are allergic to. You may have noticed patterns of skin or digestive reactions when you are exposed to or ingest certain things. When dowsing, you must put your guesses to the side completely, or your dowsing will be inaccurate. There is no point dowsing just to justify your guess. That isn't dowsing.

Be sure to be in a proper dowsing state when dowsing this question:

On a scale of 0 to 10, with 0 being no reaction and 10 being the worst allergic or sensitivity reaction, how allergic or sensitive am I at this time to _____(name the substance)? 0? 1? 2? Etc.

Bear in mind that you need to test individual ingredients, not prepared foods with many ingredients. If you are wanting to test a prepared food, you can ask this:

On a scale of 0 to 10, with 0 being no reaction, am I allergic or sensitive to any ingredient or combination of ingredients in this product?

We include the phrase 'combination of ingredients', because people sometimes have no reaction to a single item, but certain foods in combination do trigger a response.

We suggest you get a second opinion on all health dowsing before taking any action. But if you are a good dowser, and you get 8 or higher, it would be wise to avoid that substance until after you consult a professional.

~

61. Level of hydration

Your body is mostly water. Water is the stuff of life. Dehydration has been shown to be the cause of many symptoms that are very unpleasant, and drinking enough water can be restorative to health.

Not all water is created equal. Tap water has many toxins and contaminants in it. Even well water can have toxins like arsenic. It's important to drink the right amount of pure water each day to keep your body balanced and healthy. But how much is right for you? Each person is unique, and the standard 6-8 glasses recommended by most experts is only a starting point.

Dowsing can be used to measure how appropriately hydrated your body is. Using a scale of +10 to -10, with 0 being perfectly balanced, and positive numbers too much water and negative numbers meaning dehydrated, you can dowse what level of hydration your body has at any given time.

On a scale of +10 to -10, with 0 being perfect hydration for my body, and negative numbers meaning dehydration, what is the level of hydration of my body overall at this time? Is it a positive number? 0? A negative number? Then dowse further…Is it between -5 and -10? Etc.

As with all health issues, get confirmation before taking drastic measures. As a rule, people in our culture tend to be dehydrated, but each person is unique.

~

62. Liver function

You can dowse the function of any organ or system you wish. The liver is a vital organ and protects you from toxins, so it is important that it functions well. You can use a scale of 0 to 10 to determine how well yours is functioning, with 0 being terrible and 10 being excellent. You will notice the question uses the word 'physical', because all organs will have an energetic aspect, and sometimes what they are dealing with energetically is very different from their physical function. But most people are more concerned with the physical.

On a scale of 0 to 10, with 0 being terrible function and 10 being excellent, what is the level of physical functioning of my liver at this time? Greater than 8? Between 3 and 8? Less than 3? Keep dowsing until you get the number.

You can also use this question to measure progress (or the reverse) by changing the time frame and asking for the level of functioning on this date a month or year ago, etc.

~

63. Predicting outcomes

Would it be easier to quit smoking or eating sugar if you knew in advance that it would make your health immensely better than if you did not? Of course it would!

There are many ways to approach this. Again, we will use scales, because a simple 'yes' or 'no' won't be motivational. The 0 to 10 scale in this case could be regarded almost like percentages, if you wish. And you can change the time period to give yourself a true estimate of how long you'd have to wait for full results as well as how amazing they will be (or not).

Predicting the future is not an easy thing. In fact, it is so hard, we left it to a much later section in general. Combine health and prediction, and you have a subject that is very hard to be detached about. But it is good practice and won't hurt you at all to do this exercise. And you can mark a calendar with your question and answer and see how accurate it is.

Think about what you are intending to give up. Is it cigarettes, alcohol, sugar? Then ask this question:

On a scale of 0 to 10, with 0 being no change, how much improvement would I have in my physical health overall in _____(name a time period, like one year) if I completely gave up_____(name the substance)?

Now mark your answer down, and ask the question using a variety of time periods, always marking your answer. As you see, at some point, you will reach the highest number, and it won't always be a 10. Maybe you could get a 10 by quitting smoking, but cutting out sugar only gives you a 5 at most, no matter how long you do it. However, anything over a 3 should give you noticeable results of some kind.

∼

64. Testing diets

We don't believe in diets. We believe in healthy lifestyle choices. We don't believe in depriving yourself and hating yourself or what you want or the way you look. Diets can be a great excuse for judging and hating yourself, and we strongly disapprove of those things.

However, if you want to find a way of eating, a lifestyle that will be enjoyable while helping you reach your health goals, that is a great thing to dowse about. At the time of this writing, we are following a paleo lifestyle, having removed grains, dairy and legumes from our diet. We cheat a bit on the dairy and legumes now and then, but only rarely on the grains, because the huge difference we've seen by eliminating grain offsets completely any sense of deprivation.

Think about your goals for considering whatever diet or eating lifestyle you are thinking of adopting. You can use dowsing to evaluate its potential for helping you reach those goals and also use dowsing to predict how likely you will be to enjoy staying on it long term.

Now, you may not be intending to stay on the diet long term, and that's ok. But if you are, dowsing will help you see how hard that will be. Dowsing helps you to enter a program with eyes wide open.

On a scale of 0 to 10, with 0 being ineffective, how effective would the _____(diet or eating program) be for my health/beauty/whatever goals? More than 8?

If I adopt the _____(diet or eating plan) for _____(name a period of time), how easy and enjoyable will I find it on a scale of 0 to 10, with 0 being hard and 10 being easy? Less than 8?

8 is the number we use at the cutoff for taking action. If enjoyment is a 3, likely you won't be able to stay on it without tremendous motivation and will power, and it's highly likely you will drop it as soon as you reach your goal.

∾

65. Testing an exercise regimen

Different strokes for different folks…In "Eat Right 4 Your Type", Peter D'Adamo talks about how different blood types benefit from different types of exercise. My type likes gentler forms of exercise like yoga. Other types do better with more strenuous forms of exercise. You don't have to buy the book to find out what's best for you. You can dowse.

In particular, think of a form of exercise you are contemplating, and what purpose you have for it. For example, you might want to consider taking yoga to relax and increase your flexibility. So dowse this:

Will taking an 8 week yoga class at _____(name the location or class itself) increase my flexibility and relaxation to the degree I have in my goals? (You could also ask if it would noticeably or significantly increase your flexibility and ability to be relaxed. Or you could use a scale of 0-10 to measure the degree of change you would see.)

If you get a strong 'yes', enroll in the class and see what happens. You may need to ask about taking 3 months of yoga or a different class to get the 'yes' you want. You may substitute any form of exercise in this question.

$\sim$

66. Need a chiropractor?

Until I moved to AZ, I had the bias (common where I came from) of thinking of chiropractors as quacks. As it turned out, they have done me far more good than allopathic physicians ever did. I was plagued by terrible neck, shoulder and head pain for years. I had had a number of head traumas including a car accident before seat belts when I was 10, in which I smashed some teeth. It had never occurred to me that my spine was out of alignment and perhaps causing me pain.

If you have had an accident that could have misaligned your spine, that misalignment could be the cause of your pain. If the accident was recent, you are lucky. Fixing it now will be easier than doing it decades later like I did. And it will take less time and money.

Dowsing can be used to see if the pain you now have could be relieved, and how much it can be relieved, by the appropriate number of chiropractic adjustments with the right doctor. If you have been going along in this book as intended, working your way from the start, you will see a lot of possible questions could be dowsed here. We won't do them all. You could pick a doctor or chiropractic technique using dowsing that will be most effective for your issue. In this section, we will only ask about whether treatment will resolve the pain, and how much. You can form your own additional questions by consulting other sections in this book that help you choose methods and professionals to do the rest.

On a scale of 0 to 10, with 0 being no help, how much will chiropractic adjustment by the right person using the right method for the right number of

treatments be for relieving the cause of the pain in my neck/lower
back/wherever? Will it be 8 or more?

We don't invest in things that rank lower than an 8. If you get an 8,
create other dowsing questions to find the doctor or method, then see
if you can dowse how many appointments it will take for success.

∼

67. Get a water filtration system?

Water is vital to health. Getting enough water. Drinking pure water.
Tap water is not healthy. It contains many things that it should not.
You've probably read online about it. So you've decided you'd like to
filter your water. You might even decide to do this if you have well
water, because some well water has natural contaminants like arsenic.

There are many types of filtration systems, from simple to complex,
from cheap to expensive. Most require at least basic maintenance like
changing filters regularly, or they won't work well. Dowsing is perfect
for questions like this. While salesmen want you to think there is
always a one-size-fits-all solution to any problem, dowsing can balance
all the unique aspects of your situation and help you find the best
choice.

Consider your goals. You want pure water, the best you can afford.
You may have a particular contaminant or toxin you want to filter
out. If so, put that on the list of goals clearly. You have a budget, so
add that as a factor. You want to consider not only the initial
investment, but the cost of maintenance in terms of time, effort and
money. For example, we had a reverse osmosis system years ago, and
we hired a guy to come in at proper intervals to maintain it. Now, we
live on property with a well, and the water is pure, but it has
minerals in it, so we use a pitcher filter for water that is put in the
Keurig.

Once you have a list of your specific needs and goals, you can dowse each option you have researched for how appropriate it is for reaching all your goals, including staying within your budget:

On a scale of 0 to 10, with 0 being useless, is the _____ *(name system or option) greater than an 8 overall for my goals?*

You can also ask what the overall number is, if you want to compare several. Choose the one with the highest overall number. We usually recommend not purchasing anything that isn't an 8 or higher.

68. Heart health

Heart disease is common among those living in Western society. It can be difficult to diagnose for women. While conventional doctors focus on a few factors like cholesterol readings, heart health is actually a much more complex subject. As with all physical problems, it's best to catch heart issues early on and treat the cause, not the symptom. Dowsing can help you monitor the health of your organs and systems.

The tricky bit about using a scale for this is what are you comparing your heart function to? Is it valid to compare it to how it was working 10 years ago? Should you assume function will decline with age? Would you get a better reading if you compared yourself to a group, like all women? Or a narrow group, like all women your age living in your country? But then, what if that group actually isn't that healthy? Is that the baseline you want to use?

When dowsing, scales deliver detailed information. But you need to be thinking very clearly how you define your scale. It might be fun to change the scale and record the numbers you get and see if they are different, and try to guess why they might be the way they are.

For example, if you compare your heart health on a 0 to 10 scale with women your age in Japan, where heart disease is low, you might get a lower number than if you compare it using the same scale with women your age in the U.S., where heart disease if fairly common. Think of it this way. The 10 for women in Japan will be a more fit rating than the 10 for the U.S.

Usually we like to keep things simple, so you might do that by using a 0 to 10 scale that has the 10 be the most fit your heart could be at this time given your age and all other factors. Because you can't do better than a 10 for YOU. But you might get a bit more information that would have you thinking about visiting a doctor if you compare yourself to another group of people. It's your choice.

On a scale of 0 to 10, with 10 being the best possible function my heart can physically have at this time given all appropriate factors, is it functioning at 8 or higher?

8 or better is the number we like to see. If it is lower, you can then dowse various ways to help it, like a change in diet, more exercise, supplements or seeing a professional.

69. Choosing a health care practitioner

This one could not only save you a ton of money. It could save you pain. It could even save your life. Not all professionals are created equal. You want, no, you *need*, to find the right person to help you resolve your problem. And you want to resolve it quickly, easily, as comfortably as possible, with few or no negative side effects, at the right price and leave you healthier as a result.

Don't just mindlessly go to a doctor and ask him to remove your symptom. Be very clear about what you desire as a result. Writing down everything that matters to you will help you get your head around it.

Do some research. You can just go to the listing for doctors in the yellow pages, but you might want to do a bit of research first. If your problem is back pain, you might want to research chiropractic, massage and other holistic resources in addition to an allopathic physician. Take your beliefs and goals into account. If you don't like taking pain pills, or you would shy away from surgery, a more holistic route might suit you better.

Whatever your beliefs, give yourself options that feel right based on your condition and goals. Make a list of the professionals you would be willing to consult with for your problem. This process works whether you have allergies, back pain or any other physical issue that you want to resolve.

Sadly, money is always going to be a factor. Massage could help you a lot, but it probably isn't covered by insurance. Some holistic methods will require that you pay out of pocket. But your biggest priority is to get the best health care you can afford.

You could just dowse the list of options without making money a factor. That would tell you which professional can help you the most. If it turned out that her fees were too high for you, maybe you could get help from a family member for covering them. On the other hand, if you dowsed she was a 9 and another option was an 8, and you could afford the 8 just fine, why not go with the 8? One point is not a big enough difference to put yourself into debt, is it?

You decide whether money is a factor, or whether you'd like to make a clear, rational decision about the money after you dowse overall who is best on all the other factors. It's up to you.

Another factor that is often overlooked by spiritual people is that you will get the best results if you work with a health care professional who respects your point of view and is interested in your participation in the process. We suggest you include this as an important factor in your list of goals.

*On a scale of 0 to 10, with 10 being the best, how does*_____*(name the practitioner) rate overall for all of my goals concerning resolving*_____*(name the issue)?*

Compare the numbers of each professional and choose one that ranks 8

or higher. If none rate an 8 or higher, go back and do some more
research and add more names to the list.

70. Medicine side effects

Prescription meds have side effects, some of them worse than the
problem you are trying to cure. Even holistic remedies sometimes have
side effects. You can be allergic to a herb or a prescription med.

You can do a search online (and should) before taking any prescription
medicine. Sometimes doctors are not totally up to speed on this
subject, because new medicines come out so fast, and they have limited
time to study. Take charge of your health by doing your due diligence
and not leaving it to someone else. If you find that what you discover
makes you concerned about taking the medicine, talk to your doctor. If
your doctor is someone whose ego bruises easily, perhaps you need a
new doctor.

Here's a story about how important it is not to give your power away:

When my Dad was 97 and in the hospital due to pneumonia, one of his
doctors found out he had cold agglutinin disease, which is a form of
hemolytic anemia triggered by cold. This nonlethal condition was one
he contracted decades before. The doctor was made aware of this fact,
because my Dad's condition made it nearly impossible to draw blood
and test it, as it coagulated the minute it got out of the body. It was not
why he was in the hospital. The pneumonia was his problem.

The doctor decided to order my Dad a round of chemotherapy,
because he thought that might be an interesting way to try and offset
the symptoms of his blood condition. (Though it's impossible to know
for sure what someone's motivation is, it is worth noting that the use
of chemotherapy, unlike most of what is done in the hospital, has huge
financial benefits for the doctor ordering it, or at least did at that time.)

He never explained the process to my Dad, nor did he ask permission from my Dad or anyone in the family before ordering chemotherapy.

My sister was sitting in the room when the doctor came and announced to my Dad that they would be sending him upstairs for a new treatment. She immediately called me on the phone; I googled the medicine, which she had had to chase him down and demand the name of, and I told her to stop them right away. The medicine was contraindicated for geriatric patients. (I think 97 is elderly, but apparently the doctor wasn't concerned.) The description said death was a side effect, among many other serious ones. Of course, it was not a treatment for pneumonia, and giving it to a 97-yr-old man with a lung infection was about as responsible as playing Russian roulette—at least in my opinion.

We put a stop to the action and made a complaint to the hospital, but of course, nothing major was ever done to the doctor for his amazingly insensitive, dangerous, egotistical and might I add, stupid plans. If my sister hadn't been there and hadn't called me, my Dad almost certainly would have died due to that treatment. You need to stay on top of things and not just 'trust' the doctor. Your health is your responsibility, and no one cares more about it than you. The same is true of your life.

Back to the subject: Once you are settled on a medicine from the rational viewpoint, then you can dowse about side effects, because obviously, not everyone experiences side effects the same. You want to make sure that your body won't have a serious reaction. My Mom was allergic to antibiotics. She would break out in hives. Her reaction was worse with certain classes of antibiotics, but pretty much all antibiotics gave her a reaction, which made it hard to treat infection conventionally. Don't ignore side effects, and use dowsing to find out in advance so you can avoid serious ones. If your doctor won't believe your dowsing, get a new doctor. Your health is your greatest gift. Don't squander or risk it.

On a 0 to 10 scale, with 0 being no side effects and 10 being the worst I could experience, what level of side effects will I see if I take _____(name the medication) at the prescribed dosage for as long as the doctor wants me to?

Usually, a 3 or higher will give noticeable side effects. A lot depends on the person. I wouldn't want a 5 or higher, but I definitely would not take any medicine that ranked 8 or higher, as it could be dangerous.

This is an example of an advanced health dowsing application. If you jumped ahead in the book, you probably lack the experience and detachment needed to get a good dowsing answer on this question. Fear must be put aside when dowsing, as it causes inaccuracy. If you feel fear when dowsing, don't dowse. As always, get a second opinion before taking action.

∾

71. Testing elective surgery

You can dowse any type of proposed surgery for how effective it will be for its stated purpose, but in this exercise we will address elective surgery. We suggest that you also dowse the level of side effects of any proposed surgery and the speed of recovery after it. Those factors might cause you to reconsider an elective surgery, and knowing what's likely to happen can allow you to prepare to deal with it.

Sometimes a surgery will dowse poorly at this time, because your body is not up to handling the stress and the recovery. Or maybe there are other factors at work, like if you did it as planned, it would take place during a fire or earthquake or power outage that would endanger you. The point is, that getting a low number now only means now. You can always try a later date.

On a scale of 0 to 10, with 0 being useless, how effective will_____(name the surgery) be for my goals if I have_____(name the doctor) perform it in_____(name the time frame)?

By adding the surgeon and time frame, you are more specific and will get a better answer. Your body has its ups and downs, and you want to choose a good time frame. Plus you obviously want a good surgeon. If the number is less than 8, reconsider the various factors, including whether you really want the surgery.

72. Select a holistic remedy

Self-care is wonderful. Prevention is terrific. But you probably don't have a lot of experience with all the holistic remedies you can use. Even if you are an intuitive person, standing in the health food store staring at flower essences, homeopathics and essential oils can be overwhelming. In addition, your limited experience may cause you to narrow your search, and that could lead to you not using the best remedy. We all tend to be drawn to what we know. It gives us comfort.

There's nothing wrong with that, but dowsing will help you know if expanding your search is important for reaching your goals. As always, write your goals down. All of them. Then dowse a list of remedies you would be willing to purchase and use.

Is_____(name the type of remedy) an 8 or higher on a scale of 0 to 10, with 0 being useless, for my current health goals?

You may find they all test 8 or higher, but put aside the methods that do not. Then you can ask the same question again for those that tested 8 or higher, but substitute 10 and see what you get. If none test at 10, try 9. Go with whatever method tests highest.

Then you need to find the exact remedy among all those offered. Say you got flower essence as the best. You would then ask:

Are any of the flower essences on this shelf/in this catalog listing an 8 or higher on a scale of 0 to 10 for the goals I just wrote?

If you get 'no', that's because the flower essence you need is not on that shelf or listed in that catalog. You have a choice to go look elsewhere for the right flower essence, or start over and pick another type of remedy that has what you need right here, right now.

Sometimes you will see better results with a combination of essences, rather than just one. You can dowse:

Is there a single flower essence here/listed that will be an 8 or higher for my written health goals at this time?

If 'yes', then you list dowse or point your finger at each one and ask the question:

Is this the best flower essence for my written health goals at this time?

Asking this way will get you the best one quickly. But you could rank each of them if you want.

If you got 'no' to the question about a single remedy, ask if there are 2 taken together that are 8 or higher. Then dowse to find which 2 they are. Do your best to trust your dowsing and record your results.

Dowsing in a store can be distracting. It's important to get into a dowsing state, so if you jumped ahead in the book, be aware you might not be ready to do this exercise.

73. Test for allergens in food

A lot of people have food allergies. If you are one of them, you do your best to avoid allergens. But it can be a real challenge to eat in a restaurant or go to dinner at a friend's house. Or to participate in the family reunion picnic or potluck at church. You don't want to be asking everyone if garlic (or whatever) is in that dish.

Here's where dowsing is a real help. You can't easily know all the ingredients using rational means.

Is there any _____(name the allergen) in this dish/menu item?

Simple. Don't eat anything that tests as having the allergen. However, this type of dowsing requires a level of experience you may not have if you skipped ahead in the book and haven't practiced getting into a dowsing state and being detached.

Do not use dowsing as your only tool to protect yourself from anaphylactic shock. If you have a serious allergy, ask the person who prepared the dish. Nothing is 100%, and your health is too precious to risk.

~

74. Do you need a doctor?

Do I need a doctor? Seems a simple question, but it isn't. Taking time off from work, driving or being driven to an ER or doctor's office and paying for a visit as needed can be a real nuisance.

There are times when it's obvious you must go to a doctor. An example would be serious trauma of any kind or an infection that has gotten out of control. There are times you know you don't need to see a doctor. A cold or simple allergies can be handled with simple remedies you have on hand or can get at the drug store.

It's the in-between situations that give you pause. They don't happen all that often, do they? But they force you to guess. If you are an extra cautious person, you may choose on those occasions to go to the doctor. After it's over, you might kick yourself and feel it wasn't needed. Or you might be the opposite. Maybe you tend to be too brave, and you don't go when you really should, and that allows matters to get worse. In other words, you just don't know what to do in some situations. You cannot rationally know.

Dowsing is a super resource at times like this. This is a perfect situation for programming a simple question. When you are injured or sick, or have an injured or sick pet or child, you won't want to take the time to make a list of goals and then ask a complex dowsing question. What we have done is follow the programming instructions in the earlier section of this book, and when a situation comes up where we aren't sure about seeking outside help, we dowse the programmed question:

Should I consult a doctor about this?

We never use 'should' in typical dowsing questions, as it implies a judgment, and judgments make things fuzzy, but for a programmed question, it's ok.

Do NOT dowse this question until and unless you have followed the programming steps that include making a detailed list of all your goals. See the section on Programming Your Question earlier in the book for instructions.

We have never, ever been steered wrong since we started using this method. In the year previous to writing this book, we have had 4 of our 8 cats have trauma that was serious enough that we weren't sure we could handle it without help. In every case, we dowsed that we could handle it, so we didn't go to the vet. And in every case, they got well just fine using the home remedies we had at hand. Each case probably saved us at least $300. Now, we aren't saying money should be the priority, but we want to show you that accurate dowsing will save you money.

The same will be true if you go to the doctor if that is what you dowse. Not going to the doctor when you should will create more problems that will be more costly in the end.

This type of dowsing should NEVER be done by newbies. And as always, get a second opinion. Dowsing is not 100% accurate. Nothing is. We have a built in second opinion, because we both dowse any important subject independently. And we are conservative in that if one of us gets 'go to the doc', we will go. Don't take chances or risk anyone's health.

Let's end this subject by pointing out a fact you may not have thought about: if you don't dowse this subject, you have to guess.

Guesses are not accurate, either. In fact, guesses will be less accurate than dowsing. So don't be afraid to dowse, because dowsing increases your chances of being right. But use care and always get a second opinion, and don't dowse over your level of competence.

~

75. Measure EMF effects

EMFs (electromagnetic frequencies) are a health issue for many people. You may not even be aware that your exposure to certain EMFs is the cause of your physical symptoms. There are meters you can buy or rent that will test various types of EMFs in your home. If you suspect you have a problem, it is wise to do a survey this way. But there are many types of EMFs that are not easily measurable at this time, so dowsing is a good tool to add to the process.

You can check your cell phone, your microwave and your router, as they are 3 common problems. You probably should check the effects of your clock radio if you have one near your bed and your TV if you have one in the bedroom. Don't forget your phone charger or dock, either.

You can use the same question to test the effects of each:

On a scale of 0 to 10, with 0 being no effect and 10 being the worst negative effect, what is the level of effects on my physical health of the EMFs associated with_____(name the item) in the way I am currently using it and in the location(s) it currently has?

8 or higher requires action of some type. You can do research to find the best way to resolve things. Unplugging your router at night can help with that. If your microwave is leaking radiation, get a new one. Move the TV out of the bedroom and get a wind-up alarm clock. Don't carry your cell phone in a pocket. There are protective devices and methods you can research online as well.

76. Are you pregnant?

Some dowsers are really good at this question. You may want to ask about your horse, your dog or yourself. For this exercise, we'll assume you are testing yourself. This is a good exercise to do before using a pregnancy test from the store. That way, you can confirm your results. Remember that many early pregnancies are lost, and the mother is unaware of having been pregnant, so if you want to confirm your dowsing, try to do the test soon after you dowse.

Am I pregnant at this time?

You can obviously use dowsing to determine the number of babies you will give birth to and their gender. You could also use dowsing to try and predict the date you will deliver, if you are having a natural birth. Likewise, dowsing will help you make various other birthing choices to help make the process easier.

One of the more popular forms of dowsing was using a wedding ring on a thread to determine the sex of the unborn child. It was used a lot, although hardly anyone called it dowsing!

9

Choices About Home

77. Moving

It is a big decision, moving to a new location. It can affect all areas of your life. You want a move that will increase your happiness and success on all levels. Make a list of goals you have for considering a move. Do you want to have improved health? Finances? Health? Be sure the list is complete, and note which ones should be given greater weight.

Do your due diligence researching places you think might suit you and make a list of the top several locations. Don't skip this. The earth is a huge place. Use your left brain and try to find some locations that you believe would be suitable, then use dowsing to refine your choice. As with all major choices, be sure to get a second opinion.

On a scale of +10 to -10, with 0 being neutral and negative numbers meaning a bad experience, how does _____(name location) rank overall for my goals as a place to move to in _____(give a time frame)?

Or you could just ask:

Is_____(name location) at least a +8 overall for my goals on a scale of +10 to -10, with 0 being neutral and negative numbers being a bad experience, if the move takes place_____(name a time frame)?

We use 8 as a cutoff for taking action. If none of the places are 8 or better, then it could be your time frame is off. Or maybe you need to find some more locations to test.

If there is only one point difference between places, you might want to test each item in your list of goals for the locations, to see how it rates for each goal. That might help you choose. One could be excellent for your finances, while the other might be lower, and if that is a big goal, you need to know that.

∼

78. Rent a house or buy

Which is best for your needs? Rent a house or buy one? If after using your rational mind carefully and considering all your goals, you still aren't sure, dowsing can help you make a good choice. Have a complete list of your goals and priorities and then dowse.

You will find it useful at times when faced with two choices to first dowse if there is any significant difference between the two. If not, just pick one. If there is, then proceed with dowsing.

For my goals, is there any significant difference in outcomes overall between renting a home and buying one at this time?

How does renting a house rank on a scale of 0 to 10 overall for my goals at this time, with 0 being terrible and 10 being excellent?

How does buying a house rank on a scale of 0 to 10 overall for my goals at this time, with 0 being terrible and 10 being excellent?

As always, we use 8 as a cutoff point for taking action. If neither rates 8 or higher, you might want to consider other options, like a condo or apartment.

79. List price for selling

This is always a tricky question. You want to get the most from the sale of your home, but the real estate agent is eager for a fast sale, and sometimes she will recommend a price that seems very low to you. It could be that she is correct, and she can provide comps to show you. If there is a big difference between her suggested listing price and what you want to list it at, that can create a lot of anxiety.

Definitely do your due diligence and look at comps and discuss the matter carefully. Don't let the fact that you need or want a certain sale price cloud good judgment. Having the house hang on the market forever is a bad thing all around.

We had to sell my mother's house when she went into hospice, and the market was so bad that it was worth half as much as it had been worth several years earlier. We wanted to sell it fast, because it was empty and costing us money. But we didn't want to give it away. Yet in looking around the area, we could see just how hard it could end up being if we asked too much.

We asked my best friend to dowse a price for us, and we also dowsed. It was much lower than we had hoped for. But it wasn't a giveaway. It just wasn't a great price. We went with the dowsing, and the house sold in less than 2 weeks. We were convinced that the buyer would not have taken it at a higher price, and maybe if she had not bought, it would have lingered on the market like hundreds of houses have.

Our needs in that situation meant we had to sell as fast as possible, because the house was costing us money and we lived 100 miles away. Your needs could be different. Make a list of the things that matter most to you in selling your house. What are your exact goals? Then do the research about sales in your area. Get an estimate on the house. Form a reasonable idea of what you think is a good price for your goals. Then dowse:

Is_____(asking price) an 8 or higher on a scale of 0 to 10 overall for my goals at this time, with 10 being best?

If the answer is 'no', you can replace the asking price with other numbers, noting the rank you get for each. When you get an 8 or higher, you can look at your list of goals and dowse how that price ranks for each goal. It might be that it is great for selling the house fast, but not as good for getting a good price. You will have a chance to adjust based on your dowsing. Maybe if dowsing says that 2 prices are 8 and 9, with one being better for a fast sale and the other for profit, you can decide which matters most to you and go with the appropriate price.

10

Career, Education & Business

80. Evaluate a job offer

You have a job offer, and it looks pretty good, but you just aren't sure whether to take it. Maybe you are hoping for another offer to come from a company you like better, or with a better salary, or doing something you like more. Or perhaps you are just unsure, even though you aren't expecting any other offers. You wonder if maybe you should look some more.

Dowsing can be very useful in this situation. It can be used to verify that 'gut feeling' you are having, or to open the door to a new way of looking at things.

Make a list of the things you want in a job. Be specific and detailed. Remember to include more than money, status and size of office. Include your goals for relationships with your boss and co-workers, chance for advancement or travel, the opportunity to be creative, etc. Then dowse:

On a scale of 0 to 10, with 0 being terrible and 10 being excellent, how does this job I am currently being offered rank overall for my list of goals at this time? 10? 9? 8? Etc.

Or you can just ask:

Is this job offer at least an 8 overall on a scale of 10 for my list of goals at this time?

If the job is not an 8, you can dowse each item on your list and find out where the weaknesses lie. If it ranks high on your biggest goals, perhaps you will want to remove the low-ranking items from the list and re-dowse to see if the offer is now 8 or better. But we warn you that compromise is a slippery slope, and you are better off sticking to your goals and finding a job that meets them all, if you want to be happy.

~

81. Find an accountant

If you are in business, you need an accountant, at least for doing your taxes. You want to find one who not only is competent, but has certain other traits. Obviously, he must have honesty and integrity. Maybe you'd also like him to be able to give you good advice on certain decisions. Make a list that is detailed and specific of the goals you have in mind for hiring an accountant. If price is a factor, add it to the list. Once you have the list done, you need a list of candidates.

We actually did this exercise years ago when we needed to hire a new accountant to replace our old one who was retiring. We went to the yellow pages and did some dowsing after getting our goals clear. We couldn't be happier with the accountant we chose. He is amazing, honest, intelligent and very open-minded about what we do for a living. He's pleasant and always has a happy demeanor. We love him. And we found him through dowsing. You can do the same.

Make a list of the names you wish to consider.

Is anyone on this list an 8 or better on a scale of 0 to 10 overall for my goals at this time, with 0 being terrible?

If you get 'no', find a way to add names to the list. If you get 'yes', then go down the list and ask, as you say or point to a name:

Is this one an 8 or higher?

Note all the ones who make the cut, then get an actual ranking for each. You might also want to take the highest ones and dowse them as to how they rate on the individual goals you have in your list.

If 2 are very close, you definitely want to dowse you list of goals to find out the strengths and weaknesses of each so you can choose better.

~

82. Choosing a business name

The name of your business is very important. It should reflect what you are offering clearly to those who are your market. Hopefully it is attractive and grabs their attention. Your business name should never be like the first one we chose for our business. Our first choice was ridiculous. It was unclear what our business was about, and it made no sense and had no attraction at all. Want to know what it was? *Walking 3 Paths.* Huh?

Yeah, that doesn't mean anything, does it? *Sixth Sense Consulting* makes a lot more sense. It also had the advantage of growing with us, fitting our business as it evolved and we offered different types of products and services. Our current business name, *Sixth Sense Solutions,* is even better at describing what we now offer, since we discontinued consulting services.

You may have an idea of what you'd like to call your business. But you aren't sure. It's a big choice and hard to change. So make a list of all the things you want your business name to do. Include attracting clients and being able to adapt to your business offerings as your business grows and evolves. You want a name that is clear to your potential market and not the same as or even close to the name of a competitor. It should be easy to spell, so people can google and find it.

Once you have the list, make note of the names you are considering and dowse each to rate them for how well they will meet your list of goals now and in the future.

On a scale of 0 to 10, with 0 being terrible, how does_____(business name) rate overall at this time for meeting the goals I have listed for a business name?

You want to go for an 8 or higher. If none rate even near an 8, go back to the drawing board.

Always ask for a second opinion on important choices like this.

∿

83. Evaluate a business opportunity

Going into business is a big deal. Having spent years in a variety of businesses, we can tell you that one of the most important things to consider is whether you can picture yourself doing this for many years. Make a list of your goals, and include money and time and success and happiness and everything else you want from being in business. Then dowse the opportunity to see how it rates.

Is_____(business opportunity) an 8 or higher overall at this time on a scale of 0 to 10 for my business goals, with 0 being poor and 10 being excellent?

If it isn't an 8 or higher, you probably don't want to invest the work and time in the project. Of course, we advise you to get a second opinion on all major choices.

∿

84. How profitable?

In business, profit is an important goal. For major decisions, you will take a lot of factors into account, but with some, you already know that if it won't be profitable within a certain period of time, you aren't interested. Yet how can you know? You don't have a crystal ball. But you do have dowsing.

Predicting the future is filled with danger. Nothing is 100%, and there is no guarantee you will get the right answer. However, if you've been practicing your dowsing technique and are able to be detached and get into a good dowsing state, you might have success with this question:

On a scale of 0 to 10, with 0 being no profit and 10 being the greatest possible, how profitable overall will it be for my business in_____(name a time frame) if I_____(name the action, like start a certain project, or take on someone as a new partner, or expand into a new market)?

We generally suggest not taking action unless it dowses as 8 or better. If you like, you can change the time frame to see if that changes the answer, making it more attractive.

Please note that if you have issues around money or profit, your dowsing will probably not be accurate. And if your issues are subconscious, you won't be aware of them. See the section on Personal Growth for details.

∾

85. When to launch?

You've got a great idea for a new product, and you know about how long it will take before it's ready to launch. But you don't want to rush into launching it. You want to announce it at the best time, the time that will have the largest portion of your market focused on it with interest.

This is another future prediction with dowsing, and future prediction carries its own risks. You must have a very good question and be totally detached about what the answer might be. So think carefully what results you want to see when you launch your new project or product. Make a list. Get a time frame, like a 12-month period or a 6-month period that would suit you for launching. Then dowse:

*During*_____*(name the time frame by month, such as Jan 2017 through September 2018), is there any month that ranks 8 or higher overall for my goals on a 0 to 10 scale, with 10 being perfect, for launching my new product (name the product)?*

If you get 'no', maybe you need to re-examine your goals. Or the time frame. If you get 'yes', then you dowse and ask which months are 8 or higher:

*Is*_____*(name the month) an 8 or higher overall for my goals?*

Make a list of all the ones that are, then see if any are 10. Work your way through the list and choose the best one. You can then use the same method to pick what week in that month or even what day of that week will be best for your purposes.

∾

86. How happy will you be?

It's time to declare a major in college, or maybe to make a decision about advanced training that will put you on the path to a particular career, and you aren't dead certain whether it's a good idea. Your parents like the sound of you being a lawyer, but you've always been fond of literature.

It can be very difficult to stand up for what you want to do. Sometimes you aren't even sure what that is, making it hard to ignore the pressure of loved ones who claim to know what's best for you. Dowsing can give you refreshing information that will help you feel more confident about investing a lot of time and effort into a training or educational program.

In this case, you don't have to make a list of goals. The idea is to measure how happy you will be with the decision you made. We pick a time frame that is far enough down the road so that if asked at that time, you'd know the answer.

If I enter law school/declare my major as geology/get certified in Spiritual Response Therapy, will I be happy overall with that decision 5 years from now?

You can change the time frame to suit the decision. If you are training to be a doctor, you may have to ask if you'd be happy in 10 years' time. You can also use a scale and ask if you'd be happy at 8 or higher on a scale of 10.

11

Finances

87. Investing with Cousin Ed

Cousin Ed has approached you with an investment scheme that he believes could double your investment in six months. He isn't prone to hare-brained nonsense, but the amount of money he wants you to invest is large, and although you have some set aside, you can't afford to lose it. What do you do?

Well, it's never wise to do this sort of thing with family. If things go wrong, they can't be undone, and it can lead to horrible consequences. But you're not going to listen to me, are you? At least use dowsing to see whether it's a good investment for you.

As always, you need a list of goals. Not only to find out if his claims of profit are right, but whether this adventure would negatively impact your relationship with him, or whether it could have some unexpected negative consequences for you. Make a list of the factors that matter to you. Then dowse:

On a scale of +10 to -10, with 0 being neutral and negative being a bad result, what is the overall likely result for my goals within_____(name a time period) if I invest with Cousin Ed as he has suggested? Is it a positive number? Negative? Worse than -5?

You can change the time period if you like, to see if the answers change. But don't invest with him if it is less than +8.

You will find it hard to be detached about this, as you have all kinds of pressures to make a certain decision, and you may be infatuated with the idea as well. Detachment is vital. You don't have to follow your dowsing, but you need to be open to hearing the truth. And remember, a negative number isn't a slam at Cousin Ed. It could be that the economy or the market in that field is going to have a very unexpected shift in a bad direction that could lead to disaster. You can't know exactly what is behind a negative answer. It requires trust to go with it. So get a second opinion.

∼

88. Choosing an investment strategy

You are able to save money from your business or job, and you'd like to invest it in the wisest way for your goals. Maybe you want it to grow into a nice retirement income. Or perhaps you are saving for your children's college expenses. You may have plans about what date you want the money to be available for your use.

Make a list of all your goals. Then consult with experts and do research about what options are available to you. Once you have a selection of a few that seem pretty good, you're ready to dowse:

On a scale of +10 to -10, with 0 being neutral and negative numbers being bad results, what is the overall level in effects for my goals of investing_____(name amount) in_____(name the plan) at this time?

Never do anything that gives a negative number. We suggest not taking action unless the positive number is 8 or higher.

12

Personal Growth

89. Subconscious blocks to wealth

The subconscious rules your life, but you cannot consciously know what it believes. Dowsing is the best tool for uncovering faulty beliefs that are blocking your success in any area of life. These beliefs are often silly, even stupid, but we all have them. They were usually formed from strong emotions relating to traumas in this and other lives. By identifying and clearing them, you can make it easier to see change in your life.

This is a subject worthy of a whole weekend workshop, but here are a couple common faulty beliefs that you may have:

At the subconscious level, do I believe that being poor makes me more spiritual?

At the subconscious level, do I believe that wanting wealth is greedy?

At the subconscious level, do I believe that it will be harder to get to heaven if I am wealthy?

These are advanced dowsing exercises. You need to be merely curious about the answers, not judgmental. You must get into a proper dowsing state. If you are not wealthy and you'd like to be, chances are that you have at least one of the above beliefs.

Once you discover them, why not try and find some more. It's actually quite fun!

∽

90. How to clear blocks

Once you've revealed the naughty beliefs in your subconscious, what do you do with them? You need to transform the energy of them so that they no longer affect you. There are many ways to transform energy. All are anchored with intention. This is not an exhaustive list, but it gives you some ideas:

- Statement or prayer of intent
- EFT (Emotional Freedom Technique)
- Statement of intent with crystal, color, number or symbol
- Ritual or ceremony

Make a list of any techniques you know that can transform energy and add them to a list that also includes any of the above that you can do. Then dowse the list, asking for a 'yes' when you point at or say the best method:

Which of these is the most effective way to totally and permanently transform the energy of this subconscious belief?

Then apply the method and go back and re-test the belief. It should have cleared. If you like this subject, take a course on it. It's beyond the scope of this book to examine all the wrinkles in subconscious belief work.

Warning: Dowsing is NOT a method for transforming energy, no

matter what you may have heard. **Dowsing is for asking questions and getting answers.**

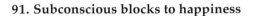

91. Subconscious blocks to happiness

Everyone wants to be happy, right? Maybe at the conscious level, but the subconscious is what rules your life, and you can't know what it's thinking unless you use a method like dowsing, because the subconscious is not accessible through your conscious mind.

Don't feel bad when you discover through dowsing that you have some subconscious blocks to being happy. Just be glad you discovered them and clear them using the instructions in the previous section. Here are just a few to test:

At the subconscious level, do I really want to be happy?

At the subconscious level, do I believe I deserve to be happy?

At the subconscious level, do I believe that if I am happy, I will die?

Unless you are deliriously happy at this time, you probably have at least one of the above beliefs. Clear them and then explore and see if you can think of other beliefs to test and clear.

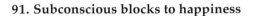

92. Subconscious blocks to a fulfilling relationship

Another common assumption is that we want to have fulfilling relationships. We don't consciously go out of our way to marry people so we can argue with them night and day. Yet sometimes it seems that way. Once again, the subconscious is running the show, and you can't know what it thinks by using your conscious mind.

But you can find out what's going on through dowsing. Here are a few common beliefs:

At the subconscious level, do I believe I deserve to have a happy, fulfilling marriage/friendship/partnership?

At the subconscious level, do I believe I must do all the giving in any important relationship?

At the subconscious level, am I willing to accept plenty of love and admiration from those close to me?

Use the clearing methods from earlier in this chapter to clear any that you find are active in you.

∼

93. How much do you really love yourself?

Probably the one root cause of all the ills in this world is that people do not love and accept themselves as they are. Then they project that judgment or hate onto others, and it spreads like a disease. You might think you totally love and accept yourself. Or maybe you know that you don't. Either way, dowsing can reveal your innermost beliefs on this subject, so that you can use whatever method you want to strengthen and build your self-love.

On a scale of 0 to 10, with 0 being not at all and 10 being the most I can, how much do I love and accept myself as I am at this time? More than 5? More than 8?

Narrow it down to get a number. You can then measure your progress as you do your self-work by going back and testing this statement.

13

Energies

94. Curses?

Yeah, we used to laugh at the idea ourselves. But after many years of working with people all over the world, we had to accept the fact that curses exist. They seem to be more prevalent in cultures that accept them as a possibility, but Western culture is definitely not free of them.

Ever cross paths with someone who had road rage and gave you the finger? That's a curse. It probably won't last that long or have a big effect on you, because the person doesn't know you and isn't putting ongoing emotion into maintaining it.

How about if you break up with your spouse, and she says she won't be happy until you die a slow, painful death? (This is from real life… we are not making this up). That is a real curse, too, but much more powerful, because each day, she stokes the fire of it and dwells on it and focuses on a very negative outcome. And it can have a great effect, especially if you have any magnets in your system, like a feeling of responsibility for her unhappiness or guilt about the breakup. The magnets can be conscious or subconscious, and they are a back door that let the curse into your system.

A curse can affect your health, wealth, business and relationships. Anyone can curse you. They don't have to be a voodoo priest (though we've seen that, too, and it is powerful). They might even be someone close to you or someone who says they are a spiritual person. It isn't just 'bad' people who curse others. It's fearful, angry, jealous, victimized and powerless people who are most likely to hurl curse energy your way.

Curse energy is more common when you are in the public eye or going through difficult personal challenges with other people. It's a good idea at those times to use dowsing to identify if any curse energy is being sent your way, and also to find out how to protect yourself. It is way beyond the scope of this book to cover this important topic, but you can use many of the same methods for protection that you do for clearing. Intention is the key.

At this time, is there any curse energy being directed at me/my business/my property?

On a scale of 0 to 10, with 0 having no effect, what is the overall level in effects of this curse energy on me at this time? Over 8? Between 5 and 8? Less than 5?

Make a list of clearing methods and then dowse which will be most effective in protecting you from this curse energy. Disempower the curse, then go back and re-dowse this question.

$\sim$

95. How are your boundaries?

Your energetic boundaries are vital for your health and protection. Many people have poor boundaries, or even no boundaries. The result is that they are affected terribly by negative energies and situations around them.

If you are overly empathetic, have a tendency to feel responsible for other people's happiness and well-being, are more of a giver than a receiver or have any past lives as a healer or shaman, you may have very poor boundaries. Strengthening your boundaries can improve your health and well-being tremendously.

Dowse the question:

On a scale of 0 to 10, with 0 being no boundaries and 10 being the strongest and healthiest possible, are my boundaries 8 or higher at this time? 5 or higher? 6? 7?

If your boundaries are less than an 8, they need some help. If they are very low, attending to them could dramatically improve your life. However, it can take time and effort to change weak boundaries.

Clearing connections to past lives can help. Clearing subconscious beliefs having to do with being affected by those around you can help. Doing visualization to strengthen your energetic boundaries or establish protection will help. Changing your attitude to one of believing you deserve to receive as much as you give, and that you are not responsible for other people's choices can also help.

Strong, healthy boundaries will help your physical and energetic conditions immensely.

96. Geopathic stress?

Geopathic stress, or noxious energies from the earth, are fairly common. Studies have shown that they are associated with ill health and even death, especially from cancer. It has also been shown that getting rid of the energies or moving away from them can restore health. So it's pretty obvious that while you can't see geopathic stress, since it's invisible, dowsing is a very useful tool for evaluating your environment.

You can ask these questions:

Are there currently any sources of geopathic stress on my property that are affecting me at 8 or higher on a scale of 10, where 0 is no effect at all?

How many sources of noxious earth energy 8 or higher on a scale of 10 have been affecting me in my residence in the past week?

Where are they located? In my bedroom? My bed? My kitchen? My favorite chair?

There are many types of energies besides geopathic stress that can be detrimental to you. If this subject interests you, please see the Resources section for a link to our books, as we have a book on space clearing that will teach you how to clear your space.

97. Toxic workplace?

If you have a job outside of home, it might be that your workplace is toxic. If you are a sensitive person, you probably already know that. You may have suppressed that knowledge, because you feel trapped in that job. But it would be wise to use dowsing to confirm your suspicions and to let you know how negative an effect your workplace is having on you, so that you can decide what measures to take.

Here are some questions you can ask:

On a scale of 0 to 10, with 0 being not toxic at all and 10 being the worst it can be for my health and well-being, how toxic is my current work environment at this time? Is it over an 8? 9? 10?

Is it possible for me to clear or transform the energies causing this?

Is there a method I know that would work for this purpose?

Will clearing the energies reduce the number to below a 3 on a scale of 10?

How often will I need to clear to keep it below a 3? Daily? Weekly? Monthly?

Obviously, this is not a space clearing course, but if you get scary answers, you might want to look into our book, *Space Clearing: Beyond Feng Shui* at Sixth Sense Books, www.sixthsensebooks.com. If you get a very high number for toxicity, but you get that you cannot clear it or clear it easily, you might want to consider finding a new job. Your health matters, and you need to make healthy choices.

~

98. Entity attachment

So this is going to sound weird. Maybe you don't want to believe in ghosts or entities. So skip this section, but do it at your peril. Entity is a general word that includes forms of consciousness that do not have physical bodies. Human discarnates, or ghosts, are entities. There are animal discarnates. There are all kinds of non-physical entities from other dimensions, from outside the earth, that can cross your path.

Entities generally are lost and disturbed. They are angry, frustrated, upset, depressed and just want to go home. When they run into anyone who has similar feelings, they often attach. The results of entity attachment vary. At the very least, if a depressed entity attaches to a depressed human, the human will become more depressed, thus leading her to be more attractive to other depressed entities. It becomes a downward spiral. That's why really negative behavior that doesn't seem appropriate can sometimes reflect entity attachment.

Human discarnates attaching to other humans can cause them to feel pain or suffering that is not their own. Long term, that can be unhealthy for the person who has the attachment.

Entities from other dimensions can be most troubling. They can sometimes lead to madness, suicide and all kinds of similar problems related to mental issues. Yes, we realize this sounds like a strange claim, but we've seen it all.

It is possible to clear entities and send them to their right and perfect place with a statement of intention in most cases. Never regard entities as demons or bad. In most cases, they have no ill will towards you, but picking a fight with them is like baiting a wounded bear. Not smart. Be compassionate and do your best not to fight. Just send them to their right and perfect place in the right and perfect way using words to that effect. Do NOT send them to the Light. You cannot and must not presume to know where they belong.

You can dowse if you or your pet or child has entities:

Are there any entities attached to _____(name of person or pet) at this time?

If you get 'yes', fashion a prayer of intention sending them to their right and perfect place in the right and perfect way. That allows the Universe to sort the details and make sure they and you are both happy.

It can be very wise to check daily for entities on your child after school, after any visit you make to a place like a hospital, bar or shopping mall, or after any unusually negative behavior is exhibited.

14

Predicting The Future

99. Will it rain?

OK, so you thought predicting the future would be more glamorous than "will it rain tomorrow?" Predicting the future is dicey at best. Even the best dowsers find it challenging. There are many theories as to why that is. At the very least, predicting the future must be regarded as a challenge to everyone. If you are new to dowsing and haven't had a really in-depth training, don't even bother trying to dowse the future.

Dowsing the future requires a level of detachment beyond what most newbies possess. That's why these are at the end of the book, even though they seem trivial. You need to be sure you are able to easily get into a dowsing state as well. And your question must be very, very clear. All of these require expert dowsing.

Even if you are a true expert, you will find pitfalls in predicting the future. It may not be your dowsing that fails or trips you up. It may be your subconscious beliefs. For example, you fail to dowse a winning lottery number because you have subconscious beliefs that say you must not gamble or win at gambling. So your system gives you incorrect answers no matter what, unless you change those beliefs. Which of course you cannot know unless you dowse about them.

Dowsing the future if it involves another person is also difficult, as you cannot control or easily predict what they choose to do with free will. So the examples here are for the most part simple, but we threw in one gambling one just for fun. If you win anything, let us know!

So we'll start with a simple question about an outdoor event your are planning. You can reword this question to predict the rain in other situations, if you like. Let's say you are having a family picnic on this coming Saturday afternoon. You could ask:

Will it rain at_____(give the address of the picnic, the complete address) on _____(give the date) between the hours of _____(list the range of hours you expect your picnic to last)?

If you get 'no', great. If you get 'yes', you may want to refine the question:

Will the rain that falls at that address on that date between those hours be significant enough to cause everyone to want to go indoors?

If 'no', then maybe it will be a sprinkle, and you can ignore it. If 'yes', you may want to provide indoor accommodations for your event, or even change the date. This is something that is easy to confirm, and dowsing accurately will build your confidence.

100. Which horse to back?

If you don't have subconscious blocks to gambling or winning money through gambling or gaining money without working for it, then you might have success dowsing which horse to back at the racetrack. Most people will find this an impossible task, because so many of us have subconscious issues about money or getting money without working for it. In addition, many of us were programmed by society, our religion and our parents not to gamble. If in spite of these warnings, you'd like to give this a try, please do so. Just don't bet too much!

You have some choices. We have observed that if you don't bet, sometimes you can predict accurately, because that eliminates the money issues. So if you want, you could try at first without betting and see how you do. However, you may still fail if your system regards gambling in itself as wrong or perilous to your soul.

You could choose to bet a small amount. That might circumvent your issues and subconscious beliefs, because you are not wagering too much. Whatever you decide to do, the question will be pretty much the same.

If you want to find the winner, check each horse listed:

In _____(name the number of the race) at_____(name the track) on _____(name the date), will _____(give full name of the horse) win the race? Define 'win' as coming in first and being officially named the winner.

You should only get one 'yes'. If you get no 'yes' answers, maybe the race will be canceled due to weather, or perhaps a horse not listed will replace one on the list and be the winner. Use your imagination to figure out why the answers turn out as they do. You can also alter the question to ask if the horse will meet any other category that could win you money, like will it place or show (or whatever the right terms are).

~

101. Frost tonight?

When we lived in Phoenix, winter came with its challenges. Usually a few times each winter, we'd get frost, and certain of the plants in the yard would need protection. We would cover them with cloth when the sun was going down and remove the cloth the next day. If you missed even once, a plant could die. Dowsing is a good tool to use when you aren't sure whether the weather forecast is correct and you want to be extra careful.

The thing about a weather forecast is that it isn't 100%, and that it can't be perfect for the microclimates in your area, so you really need to focus your intuition so as not to be disappointed. Here's a dowsing question:

Will the low temperature tonight anywhere outside on my property at_____(give your full address) go below 33 degrees Fahrenheit?

If your property is large or has microclimates or you are particularly interested in the health of one plant, like your citrus tree, make the question include those factors.

This is another great example of dowsing that you can confirm. If you find you are good at this type of future prediction, take baby steps in new directions and see how it goes.

15

Bonus

Ask, Decide, Do

Nigel came up with 3 questions that have helped us over the years. Sometimes when you want to dowse something, you get wrong answers because it wasn't really the appropriate time to ask your question.

If you are eager to dowse about something, you might want to make sure you aren't jumping the gun by asking now. Topics such as changing jobs, moving, breaking off a relationship or buying a car could benefit from this series of questions.

Is now the best time to ask?

Just dowse:

Is this the best time to ask about this subject? (Best meaning the most likely time to get an accurate answer, for reasons of timing)

If you get 'no', don't dowse. If you get 'yes', go on to the next section.

Is now the best time to decide?

If you got that now is the best time to dowse your subject, then you want to determine if once you get an answer, if now is the best time to make a decision based on that answer. Ask this question:

Is now the best time to make a decision about this subject?

If you get 'no', dowse when that time will be. If you get 'yes', move on to the next section.

Is now the best time to take action?

Now we get to the part you were waiting for. If you got 'yes' to the questions in the previous sections, ask this one:

Is now the best time to take action on this subject I just decided?

If you get 'no', you can dowse when that time will be. If you get 'yes', you're good to go.

Ask, decide and do. Three steps you can check with dowsing.

RESOURCES

 **Discovering Dowsing Course:** We offer a DVD course for all levels of experience at http://discoveringdowsing.com/dowsing-course. **Use the coupon code 'save15' to get 15% off.**

~

OUR FREE DISCOVERING DOWSING site at http://discoveringdowsing.com has free videos and articles and recorded interviews and presentations (things we couldn't include in a book).

~

SIXTH SENSE BOOKS: See all our books on dowsing and related subjects at Sixth Sense Books, www.sixthsensebooks.com.

~

OTHER EDUCATIONAL RESOURCES

Michele Fitzgerald of Senzar Learning Center in Sedona, AZ, whom this book is dedicated to, has a wealth of valuable information on topics of interest to people interested in dowsing, manifestation and the effects of electromagnetic energies. Visit her site at http://sedonaportal.com.

PLEASE LEAVE A REVIEW

We love to write; you love to read. Please help us to reach other readers by leaving a review at the site where you got this book, because the world will be a better place if more people use dowsing in their lives. Thanks for being a part of the spiritual revolution!

ABOUT THE AUTHORS

Maggie & Nigel Percy of Sixth Sense Solutions were brought together by their mutual love of dowsing in 2000. Although separated by an ocean, they discovered their lives had many parallels, and they were quick to realize that they belonged together in spite of the many obstacles. So Maggie flew to the U.K. and spent time with Nigel, and they got married and returned to the U.S. to begin their business, Sixth Sense Solutions.

For more on dowsing, visit:
discoveringdowsing.com
For other books by Nigel & Maggie Percy, visit:
sixthsensebooks.com

Made in the USA
San Bernardino, CA
24 March 2019